SIMPLE GIFTS

SIMPLE GIFTS

THE LIVES OF PAT AND PATTY CROWLEY

JOHN N. KOTRE

ANDREWS AND McMEEL, INC.
A Universal Press Syndicate Company
Kansas City • New York • Washington

SIMPLE GIFTS Copyright © 1979 by John N. Kotre. All rights reserved. Printed in the United States of America. No part of this book may be used or reproduced in any manner whatsoever, without written permission, except in the case of reprints in the context of reviews. For information write Andrews and McMeel, Inc., A Universal Press Syndicate Company, Time & Life Building, Suite 3717, New York, New York 10020.

Quotation from Sydney Carter's lyrics to the song "The Lord of the Dance" used by permission of Galaxy Music Corp., N.Y., sole U.S. agent. Copyright © 1963 by Galliard Ltd. All rights reserved.

Library of Congress Cataloging in Publication Data

Kotre, John N
   Simple gifts.

   1. Crowley, Patrick F., 1911-1974. 2. Crowley, Patricia Caron, 1913-   3. Catholics—United States —Biography. 4. Christian Family Movement. I. Title
BX4669.K62   282'.092'2 [B]   79-19077
ISBN 0-8362-3900-8

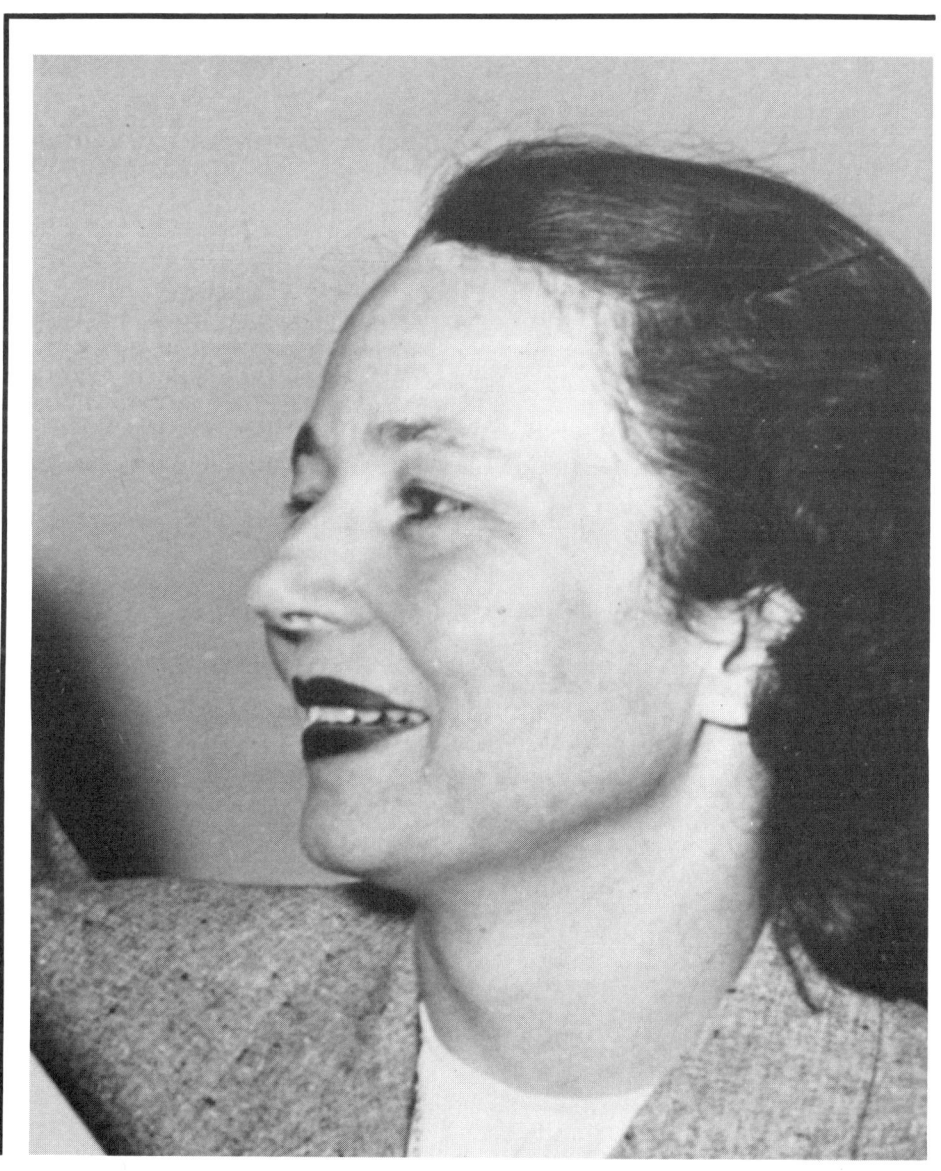

Dance, then, wherever you may be.
I am the Lord of the Dance, said He.
I'll lead you all, wherever you may be,
I will lead you all in the dance, said He.

— *from "The Lord of the Dance,"
sung to the Shaker melody, "Simple Gifts"*

Dawn breaks. A man at the face of a tomb begins to dance. Three bent and cowled figures huddling over a nearby fire turn their heads and take notice. They become agitated. One leaves the others and approaches the dancer. He is Fate, and he calls out that the dance is useless, that all is written and nothing can be changed. But the dancer does not hear. He quickens his pace and encircles Fate, and Fate is suddenly paralyzed. Alarmed, Evil straightens up, rising taller than Fate. Majestic and cunning, speaking with wisdom, power, and eloquence, he counsels despair. "Talk to me, dancer," he says. But the dancer remains silent. He twirls faster and faster, drawing tighter his loop around Evil, tangling his words, spinning him down to the earth. Then Death, the most imposing of the three, comes forth. He does not pursue the dancer but follows him with his gaze. The dancer keeps his distance, whirling slowly in a great arc. Then his eyes meet Death's, and he falters! Death smiles, but the dancer resumes, bounding higher than before, springing farther. Now it is Death who panics. He sets out in chase, trips over himself, falls to the ground and expires. The dancer leaps in triumph.

It is Easter morning.

ACKNOWLEDGMENTS

Many more people other than those named on these pages nourished and partook of the life of the Crowleys. They know who they are, they know what their place is, and they are secure in that knowledge. Only the lack of space—and the need to keep this story in focus—prevented me from speaking of them.

A number contributed in a special way to this book. The final manuscript rarely reflected the full measure of what they offered in the form of letters and taped interviews. I would like to mention them here: Sonia Kucera Anderle, Al Augustine, Burnie and Helene Bauer, Bishop Charles A. Buswell, John and Jane Clark, Jerry Crowley, Maria Pinto DeAngelis, Dorothy Drish, Helen Fagan, Monique Paul Garrity, Michele Gouard Gaudin, Collette Fernandes Gugeler, Paul Hazard, Reverend Theodore M. Hesburgh, C.S.C., Monsignor Reynold Hillenbrand, Frank Karaba, Ray and Dorothy Maldoon, Reverend Louis Putz, C.S.C., Edmund Stephan, Val Valsan, Sister Teresita Weind, S.N.D., Reggie Weissert. I learned much from the Crowley children and from Effie White, their "second" mother. Father Thomas Blantz, C.S.C., efficiently placed CFM materials in the University of Notre Dame Archives at my disposal. Professors Andre Henegers and John Noonan, Jr., offered thorough critiques of the chapter on the birth control commission. Donna Martin suggested the book's title. I first heard the story of the *Christus Victor* dancing on Easter morning from Father John Shea. I am grateful to all who assisted me and in particular to Patty Crowley, who gracefully endured long hours of interviewing, and Joseph Conners, who first approached me with the idea for this book and saw its completion through good times and bad.

CONTENTS

1. **A New Kind of Laity** 1
2. **O. J. Caron and Marietta Higman** 7
3. **Jerome Crowley and Henrietta O'Brien** 17
4. **Pat and Patty** 27
5. **Joseph Cardijn: From Belgium to Wilmette** 37
6. **The Moment** 49
7. **CFM is Born** 59
8. **The Two Worlds of Al Augustine** 73
9. **The Birth Control Commission** 87
10. **McCarthy for President** 105
11. **They Came From Many Lands** 121
12. **The Summer and Winter of CFM** 137
13. **Illness—and Familia '74** 153
14. **A Time to Die** 167
    Epilogue 179
    Notes 186

CHAPTER ONE
A NEW KIND OF LAITY

In the late 1940s middle-class American Catholics were picking up their lives after the disruption of the Second World War. They lay dormant, but their stillness was that of the countryside before it ignites at sunrise. Those who experienced that predawn quiet speak of a "mysterious archetype," of a collective readiness. Married couples had the Good Life before them but were bothered by aimlessness. They silently searched without knowing for what, without even knowing that others were groping as they.

Suddenly thousands of them found each other, and for two decades they lit up American Catholic life. Their meeting was catalyzed by a couple from Chicago pushing an idea that had come to them from the factories of Belgium. Men and women, tired of poker, bridge, luncheon, and party circuits, started going to serious meetings two and three evenings a week. They left those meetings and began calling on their neighbors, organizing projects in their schools and parishes, running conferences for engaged couples, forming credit unions, working for open housing. They took refugees, foreign students, and foster children into their homes. The women were bearing children one after another but pregnancies did not slow them down.

Their latent energies were sensed and released by one of their own kind, an "average" couple from the Chicago suburb of Wilmette. By means of a firm but unpretentious commitment to an idea—the "Inquiry Method" of Joseph Cardijn—that couple, Pat and Patty Crowley, developed an international organization of over a hundred thousand members, the Christian Family Movement. They became prototypes of the "new laity" that emerged in the Catholic Church in the 1950s. While popes called for the active participation of lay men and women, while theologians attempted to clarify the role of the laity, the Crowleys, operating on nothing but instinct, showed thousands how to assume their rightful place in the Church.

Just eight years after CFM was founded in 1949, it had spread to more than twenty countries and claimed over twenty thousand members. In June, 1957, the first meeting of its Spanish-speaking affiliate, the *Movimiento Familiar Cristiano,* was convened in Montevideo, Uruguay. In October of the same year Pius XII addressed the Second World Council of the Laity in Rome and reiterated a theme of his predecessor, Pius XI. "It would be a misunderstanding of the true nature of the Church and her social character," he said, "to distinguish in her a purely active element, the ecclesiastical authorities, and on the other hand, a purely passive element, the laity. . . . The relations between the Church and the world demand the presence of lay apostles. The *consecratio mundi* (consecration of the world) is in its essence the task of laymen, of men who are intimately involved in economic and social life, who take part in government and in legislative assemblies."[1] Later that year he bestowed the Church's *Pro Ecclesia et*

Pontifice medal on Pat and Patty Crowley. In doing so, he not only recognized CFM, but endorsed its blueprint of lay involvement in the Church.

The idea animating the Crowleys was simplicity itself: like ministers to like. Factory workers, not clergy, were to minister to factory workers, businessmen to businessmen, married couples to married couples, neighbors to neighbors. The Crowleys were "like" to a diversity of people. Pat fathered four children, adopted a fifth, and took close to fifty foster children and foreign students into his home. He was a business lawyer and, in 1968, director of the Illinois campaign of antiwar candidate Eugene McCarthy. Patty Crowley, who organized huge conferences and helped manage the McCarthy campaign, who mothered those same children and students, started her own business at the age of fifty-seven. Their role as committed laity changed abruptly in 1968 when, as members of the birth control commission called by Paul VI, they publicly dissented from his encyclical, *Humanae Vitae*. But their loyalty to the Church and the words spoken by Pius XII remained constant. After 1968 they became more universal, steering CFM in an ecumenical direction, turning their attention to the international movement, convening a series of conferences on family life, climaxed by a meeting in Dar Es Salaam, Tanzania, of representatives from all the continents and more than fifty countries.

What stands out through it all is the evenness of their inner development, the peace in the eye of their hurricane of activity. There was a single crisis in their lives together, a moment at which their trajectory crossed that of the times, their readiness matched that of the American Church. After that crisis, they steadily expanded, one action leading to the next, one link reaching out from that previous. The elemental, normal goodness that was theirs slowly gained momentum until it existed to an extraordinary degree. The cumulative effect was staggering: a network, a *family*, that covered the globe; dozens of black, brown, white, and yellow people who called them "Mom" and "Dad."

The Crowleys staked the meaning of their lives on what they did, not what they said. They were religious people, but like many of their generation, their inner lives were hidden. Pat, who died in 1974, kept a few diaries, but they were records of action rather than personal rumination. His humor, which attracted so many, which crackled through a room like an innocent prairie fire, had a way of maintaining distance even as it disarmed. For two years, through the memories of those close to him and through the written records he left, it disarmed *me* and kept *me* from his core. It was not until the end of my work, when Patty shared a few documents that "no one else had seen," that I was made aware of his inner self: of its struggles, of its hopefulness, and above all, of its simplicity.

When tragedy struck, Pat Crowley was not a Job who questioned the fairness of the universe, not a Jacob who wrestled with his God. "Whatever happens, 'tis the Lord's gentle, always acceptable will," is all he wrote. The key to Patty's life lies in an equally uncomplicated revelation, lost in hundreds of pages of transcribed interviews. At one point I was prodding her for a "deeper" explanation of her actions. She fished for something to accommodate me, and finding nothing, answered with a question of her own: "Why would you be asked? I mean you look back and it was just the hand of the Lord. All of these people coming and visiting, why did they come?"

To understand this couple and to appreciate the power of their simple gifts, one has to know the families from which they came, the climate in which they came together, and the origins of the idea that propelled them into action.

O.J. Caron at his first job, Woonsocket, Rhode Island, ca. 1904.

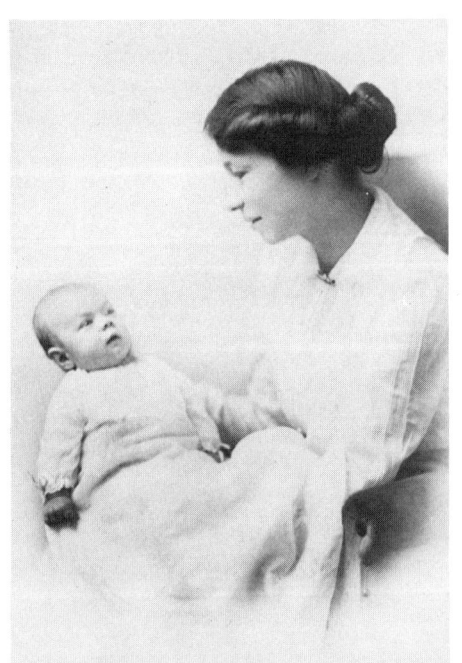

Marietta Caron and Patty, 1913.

CHAPTER TWO
O. J. CARON AND MARIETTA HIGMAN

Patty at nine (left) and at sixteen.

Sixty-five years after Woonsocket—the Carons surrounded by their family in 1969.

A church, a cemetery, and a store—nothing else—make up the town of Saint Adrian's of Ireland in Canada's province of Quebec. Of the three, it was the cemetery that commanded the eyes, the minds, and the hearts of the French who farmed the surrounding land in the 1890s. It was especially so for those whose name was Caron.

In 1892 six-year-old Ovidas Joseph Caron watched an epidemic of diphtheria take his mother, his sister, and all his brothers except the baby Adelard. Barely comprehending, little O. J. accompanied the remnants of his family to New Bedford, Massachusetts, and then to Woonsocket, Rhode Island. His father became editor of New Bedford's—and later Woonsocket's—French newspaper, but his income was meager. So O. J. often stood in food lines with a pail and waited to get his family's dole, vowing he would never again ask anybody for anything. O. J. quit the local Catholic school in the sixth grade to take a job as "affairs boy" (it meant emptying cuspidors) at Lafayette Worsted, one of Woonsocket's textile mills. Slowly he worked himself up, putting to good use the typing and shorthand he had learned from the Christian Brothers. In a few years he was the person on whom Lafayette relied to make a good impression on visitors to the plant.

At eighteen, O. J. left home to work in Philadelphia for Percy Legge, the firm that was Lafayette's sales representative, and to attend night classes at the Philadelphia School of Textile Design. Assigned small companies such as Brooklyn Knitting that no one else wanted, he soon mastered the art of salesmanship. Two years later, in 1906, O. J. went West to sell yarn for William Weinmayer. Though he was only twenty, his ambition, fed by the hunger of St. Adrian's, New Bedford, and Woonsocket, was insatiable. In one year he became the exclusive selling agent in the West for French Worsted, James Lees and Sons, and Ludwig Littauer, his territory everything on the other side of Buffalo, from Canada down to the Gulf. His home office was a small space rented from a friend in Chicago's Medinah Building.

One weekend in 1911 O. J. was introduced by a good friend and customer from St. Joseph, Michigan, to a beautiful young lady by the name of Marietta Higman. She was from *the* family of the St. Joseph-Benton Harbor area and quite attractive to this young man of humble origins. Salesman that he was, he "managed to convince her to marry me" (so he put it in memoirs scratched half a century later on a few sheets of note paper). Marietta's version of the romance is a bit different: according to the story she passed on to her daughter, she fell instantly in love with a widely traveled gentleman who intended to support her in the manner to which she was accustomed.

Marietta's father had come from a farm in Corning, New York, and made his money manufacturing wooden baskets for the fruit growers on the eastern shore of

Lake Michigan. The house he built on Lake Shore Drive was idyllic, a large white building situated on a bluff overlooking the lake, surrounded by acres of oak, mountain ash, elm, evergreen, and silver birch. It was the first house in town to have "acetylene" lights mounted on wall brackets, running water upstairs as well as down, inside bathrooms, radiators with steam heat in every room, cement walks running out to the front yard. On one side of the house were fruit trees, berry bushes, and vegetable gardens with asparagus, peas, green and wax beans, carrots, turnips, and corn (Golden Bantam and Country Gentleman were the favorite varieties). Beyond them, out by the road, was the vineyard, where a child once counted nineteen varieties of grapes, from the small "Delaware" to the large, deep blue "Concord." Between the house and the lake was an inviting expanse of lawn, beautifully kept, with swings, croquet courts, and a huge playhouse. The children's favorite spot, though, was up on the third floor—the tiny "*cupola.*" It was the perfect place to look out over the lake and wonder about life—past, present, and future.

Regardless of the weather the Higmans always went to church on Sunday. In the winter Marietta and the others were piled into an oversized bobsled and covered with warm buffalo robes. Mr. Higman, the collar of his fur coat pulled up snugly around his neck, his sealskin cap pulled down over his head, hitched up the horses and drove the family through St. Joseph and on to the Baptist church in Benton Harbor. In the spring they relied on the three-seated "democrat" for transportation, struggling over roads so muddy that the wagon wheels often sank to their hubs. In the summer the roads were thick with dust, so the children had to cover their pretty clothes with linen dusters. And in the fall the democrat was jarred by a frozen mass of ruts and clots. But whatever the conditions, never, never, did the Higmans stay at home on the Lord's Day.

Marietta came to know a father tiring from the cares and responsibilities of life. He was the man on whom both sides of the family, and much of the town, depended. He was managing his own business, overseeing his father's farm back in New York, watching a lumber interest in Tennessee, and developing 250 acres of his Lake Michigan shoreline into a public park. He had to look after Grandfather and Grandmother Barlow, to see to it that his children got to boarding schools like Exeter and colleges like Wellesley and Smith. The local school board and the Baptist church took more and more of his time. Life became "heavy," in the words of Marietta's sister; and John Higman died when Marietta was just sixteen, two years before she met her future husband.

Little wonder that Marietta's mother was stunned by her daughter's subsequent announcement that she wanted to marry a salesman—and a Catholic at that. But the girl was adamant. She had faith in O. J. and faith in her own ability to see to it that he eventually would make good. If she was lowering herself, as her mother felt, it wouldn't be for long. O. J. and Marietta exchanged vows on April 24, 1912, not with the Benton Harbor Baptists, but with a handful of Protestants, O. J.'s best friends, in a little Catholic church in Chicago. Marietta's groom was even more ambitious than she had hoped. He promptly announced that their honeymoon would be a business trip to Cleveland.

The newlyweds picked out an apartment on a small street near Lake Michigan on Chicago's North Side, just a few doors from where a family named Crowley was coaxing its son Patrick to take his first steps. The Carons did not meet the Crowleys at that time—they always seemed to move before they got to know their neighbors. Their first child, a girl, was born on July 24, 1913, and baptized Patricia in a little French church where the priest allowed Protestants—an unheard of thing—to be her godparents. Patty was followed a year later by a boy who was given the name Richard. The following summer, however, held the biggest surprise of all for Marietta Caron. When she recorded the event sixty years later, the details were still vivid in her mind.

"One hot afternoon I was out in the yard with Patty and Richard when Dad came home and told me he had an opportunity to buy a mill, Munsing Underwear, from a friend, George Rutledge, who was outgrowing his plant in Rochelle, Illinois, and moving to Chicago. He wanted to know if I would take a chance. He said he was young enough that if we weren't successful, we could start over again. Two other friends, Bob Folonie and 'Blackie' Cameron, were to put up the money and he was to run the plant. Of course, I consented and that was the beginning of Caron Spinning Company."

The following March the Carons were escorted by the mayor of Rochelle to their new home, seventy-five miles west of Chicago. "Oh, I remember that Richard, two years old, screamed from the time we left Chicago until we reached Rochelle. I remember trying to hush Richard and also trying to make an impression on the mayor. We arrived in Rochelle at 6:30 PM in a pouring rain, I think the worst I had ever experienced. Charles Collier, owner of the Collier Inn just a few blocks from the depot, met us with an umbrella. I was carrying Richard, Marietta was to be born in two months, and Patty, less than three years old, was walking. Mayor McHenry was holding the umbrella over me and Mr. Collier. Dad and a boy from the hotel were loaded with luggage.

"May 8th Dad telephoned me to come over to the mill and I pulled the first lever to start the machinery. May 15th Marietta was born.

"The last day of the year, New Year's Eve, Mr. and Mrs. Cameron and Bob and Nell Folonie spent the weekend with us. The men spent all day at the mill taking inventory and were very discouraged. The future of Caron Spinning Company looked very uncertain. We were all depressed when Mr. Cameron said, 'Well, let's all have a drink.' From that time on things didn't look so hopeless, but I remember quite a few times when Dad would telephone Mr. Cameron or Mr. Folonie to please loan him enough money to meet the payroll. Dad was spending the days on the road and he did not give up the job that he had in Chicago which was our bread and butter, two days at the Chicago office taking care of his sales, and three days in Rochelle. It was a strenuous life."

In those early years Rochelle depended for its livelihood on the Caron Spinning Company. But life there proved disastrous for Marietta Caron. She was surrounded by strangers, burdened with three young children, left alone most of the time by her husband—and was still very young. Then Patty became ill—deathly ill. Doctors in Rochelle said they couldn't help. Marietta's husband was off on a business trip. Frantic, she loaded her family on a train and rushed to a physician in Chicago. Her action saved her daughter's life, but opened a reservoir of resistance in her. She refused to return home.

So O. J. decided to operate the mill from Chicago (he was traveling most of the time anyway) and the Carons moved back to the city. But Marietta was restless, trying, it seemed, to recapture for her growing family something of what she had known as a child, to make the Carons in Chicago what the Higmans had been in St. Joseph. Soon she convinced O. J. to move to Hubbard Woods, a suburb not far from Ferry Hall in Lake Forest, where she herself had gone to boarding school. The move, however, solved none of her problems and the constant commuting from the city proved too much for her husband. The Carons' stay in Hubbard Woods was abbreviated, but before it ended Marietta had made an important decision.

At the time she was suffering from what appears to have been a nervous breakdown. To ease the burden, Patty, then eight years old, was sent to boarding school at the Sacred Heart Convent in Lake Forest. The girls there were daughters of the "right" people; the nuns were strict; and there were plenty of ribbons, medals, and processions with dainty gloves and pretty flowers. The sisters were extraordinarily kind, helping Marietta through a difficult period in her life by caring for Patty and even for her younger sister and brother. Patty's mother regained her health, but she never recovered from the charity of the sisters nor that of Father Hart of Sacred Heart parish. A year after Patty's first communion, Marietta Caron became a Catholic. It was a major step for her and a serious blow to her family.

The elite Catholicism that Marietta drew from the Sacred Heart nuns merged in the Caron family with the strict Jansenism of her husband and left strong impressions on their daughter. "I always remember, when we were little, Daddy would never go to communion unless he went to confession right before. My father always kept the rules. We went to church every Sunday, ate fish on Friday (although Daddy hated fish), and went to Catholic schools. That was our religion, really. We usually said grace only on Christmas and special occasions." Nor did the Carons ever discuss their religion. They simply kept its rules, from Lenten fasts to sexual abstinence, if no more children were desired.

After Hubbard Woods the Carons moved to a house on Astor Street in Chicago, but then moved again when it proved to be too expensive. Patty was sent to the Sacred Heart School on Pine Grove Avenue and followed its move to Sheridan Road. "It was really very exclusive. They made you feel you were better than everybody else because you were going there and getting special training. I had twelve kids in my class. Some were daughters of Irish politicians who had a lot of money. It was a real sacrifice for my father to send me to a private school like that."

Patty even flunked the fourth grade, along with four others in her class who ran into a stone wall of a nun. And something bothered her about being set apart from children who went to "regular" parochial schools. "Going to a school like Sacred Heart, you felt you were different. At the parish's children's mass I'd feel so out of place. I remember wishing I were a part of that, but I knew I was different. The kids sitting next to me didn't know me and they weren't nice to me. They never talked to me."

After eighth grade Patty was so unhappy that her mother made the drastic decision to switch her to a regular high school. "I went from a little, tiny class of twelve people to a class of several hundred. And I was thrown into this not knowing one single person, coming from a class where everybody was friendly and went to each others' birthday parties. At Sacred Heart I was somebody, but at Immaculata I was nobody and had to make my own way. I discovered another world besides people with money, and that was very, very good for me. The one friend I had there was Genevieve Gannon, who later became president of Mundelein College." But Mrs. Caron, always restless, decided that two years at a regular school were enough for her daughter. In 1930 she moved her back to Sacred Heart for her junior and senior years.

In the summer the children were always on the move. When her mother was ill, Patty, aged eight, and Richard, seven, spent several months with the elder Carons, who were still in Canada. It was an unfortunate experience. Nor were summers in Rochelle any happier. "I used to hate it, especially when I was in grammar school and high school, because I never knew anybody. And I was the daughter of the guy that owned the factory and there's nothing worse than that in a small town." But Patty loved summer camp in Rhinelander, Wisconsin—another experience arranged by her mother and paid for by extra work on the part of her father. She loved, too, all the Girl Scout activities into which her mother steered her: a summer camp in New York in 1930, a trip on the S.S. *Homeric* to Ennis Kerry, Ireland, for the 1932 Eucharistic Congress. She was one of fifteen Girl Scouts chosen to go from the States. "We could afford to pay," Patty explains, and that was unusual in the midst of the depression, but the fact that she was a Golden Eagle also may have had something to do with her selection.

Though Patty frequently left home on trips and went away to college, she never escaped the control of a mother who constantly made sacrifices for her. Patty did not want to continue with the Sacred Heart nuns after high school, so her mother selected Trinity College in Washington, D.C. When Patty traveled to Paris for her junior year and wrote home daily, Mrs. Caron had her daughter's letters typed and bound into a volume. Marietta wore herself out taking care of her children. "Education was terribly important to her. And a lot of those things we used to hate. I remember going down to the Field Museum every Saturday and watching those movies on animals. *Every* Saturday. All she did for us was what she thought was right for us, even sacrificing things for herself (which I think she did too much) for us. And she wanted us to have everything good in life.

"But she was very strict, coming from that English background and that Baptist background. There were proper things to do in society, and you just did them. It's hard to explain. I mean she was a very, very good person and everything that she did, she did for us. But she was exacting and domineering. Eventually I found out that I had to do what I thought was right even if I hurt my mother. And I really hurt my mother a lot. We had a hard time much of our life. I think she wanted to understand, but she couldn't.

"As for my father, I think one of his problems was that he was always determined to give his children as much as he could because he had had so little. He saw his mother die, and he said it was because they were poor. He always had the dread his children would be poor. He would do anything for my mother, he really would. Mother always said that if she wanted something, he'd get it if he had to work triple time to do it. She had a great influence on my father becoming the success he was. She backed him, and of course she wanted more so my father worked harder to give her more. My father was a very simple man, a self-made man.

"Mother grew up, and Dad did too, in an age when you minded your own business. I remember my father always saying that: just mind your own business. If you go along and live your own life and don't become involved, you're much better off. Once you get out and try to help somebody, you're going to get in trouble. That's the tradition I grew up in. After we got married and got involved in so many things, it was difficult for both of them because they never understood why we did it. Except when we got an award or something: Mother kept it all in a scrapbook. She had to be proud of that.

"You know, rich people often say that if you work hard you'll get there. And the reason people aren't there is because they don't work hard. Dad really felt that. But I think he also had the breaks of meeting somebody that could put some money up to buy this factory. And then he worked day and night. He worked all day Saturday, all day Sunday. He was absolutely—and my mother was, too—a good, hard, hard worker. That is why he was so proud and why it was so difficult for him to accept people who don't work. He never fired anybody in Rochelle during the depression. He just worked harder. He killed himself working.

"So I was brought up with the idea that labor unions are bad things. To this day they don't have labor unions out in Rochelle. I always hoped that we wouldn't have a union out there until my father died because it would have killed him. Mother and Dad were strict Republicans. They wouldn't have voted for God if He were a Democrat.

"At the mill Dad was often yelling at everybody; but underneath it, everybody loved him because he really had a heart. He was a big kidder. He would make people feel good even though he'd turn around and yell at them for something they did wrong. He was very nervous, very impatient, and often irritable. And you knew it was because he was tired and working too hard. He'd get really mad at us kids when we were naughty. My first brother, the one right after me, was lots and lots of trouble. So Dad had lots of tension.

"But to me he was a very soft person, a very kind-hearted person. He'd never spend much time with me, but I always enjoyed it when he came home. Being away so much, he was sometimes inclined to be a little softer. He would hardly ever say no to me. Later on, I always felt my father understood me more than my mother did, for some reason or other, even though he always backed my mother up. He never ever would go against what my mother said. He was very loyal to her—always—and that's a very admirable thing. But his feeling still came through, and I felt that maybe he didn't approve of what I was doing, but he understood. He would sometimes say, now don't get too upset about your mother. I was very close to my father."

In the summer of 1969 O. J. Caron posed for a picture at a family reunion in Rochelle, Illinois. Four generations were present. "Great-Granddaddy" sat in a lawn chair in the bright August sun next to his wife of fifty-seven years. Around him were children and grandchildren, their husbands and wives; on his lap and on Marietta's were infants whose lives would end more than a century and a half after his began. He was eighty-two, with less than three years to live. His wife would survive him by one.

O. J. had kept the vow he had made standing with a pail in a food line some seventy years before. Never had he begged for anything. He had also vindicated the idealism of a young girl by the name of Marietta Higman. She could take pride in the fact that none of her brothers or sisters had done as well as she—and, financially, she had done very, very well. Yet, even though wealth came to the Carons, it did not bring peace with it. It had been easier to fill the bucket for the first time than to erase the memory of it being empty. After all, the well could still run dry, the depression could still return, all could still be lost. In their old age the Carons knew fear, knew worry (though they had little reason to); and at times Marietta overwhelmed her children and grandchildren with all her "problems."

Nonetheless, she had survived the stress of those early years, and when her children were grown, channeled decades of energy into the American Cancer Society. Her husband had weathered heart attack after heart attack to reach this day. The tiny mill on which they staked their lives had made it through the depression and was now Caron International. All through the years, Rochelle had been a haven for the Carons from the farms in Canada. Bringing relatives and friends, they had come to O. J. in search of work, and he had provided it for them. Some of their offspring still worked at the mill. The Caron children had brought their parents joy and sorrow, pride and disgrace. Richard discovered he was an alcoholic, rehabilitated himself, founded a farm for alcoholics, and dedicated his life to it. Marietta stayed with her mother and father when they moved back to Rochelle and married late in life, only to have her husband die in a tragic accident. Joan married an ex-marine who was now a vice-president of Caron International. John, the youngest, headed the entire family business.

And Patty, the firstborn, who grew up in a home of love, tension, worry, and work, who learned the good and bad of being "proper" and "special," finally met Patrick Crowley, the toddler who lived down the street but missed her arrival back in 1913. Grandparents themselves in 1969, they stood side by side in the picture, and Pat smiled the easy smile of someone who had come before him.

CHAPTER THREE
JEROME CROWLEY AND HENRIETTA O'BRIEN

Jerome Crowley (second from right) on stage at the University of Michigan, ca. 1900.

Henrietta Crowley and her boys, Pat (left) and Jerry, ca. 1915.

Pat had his smile by the age of eight.   The Crowleys in their later years.

In the 1890s, when the Carons were recovering from the ravages of diphtheria, Treasury Agent Jeremiah J. Crowley was making ten dollars a day criss-crossing the United States in pursuit of opium smugglers. Born in Boston of Irish immigrants, he had received a degree from Georgetown in 1864 and begun a lifelong career with the Treasury. From time to time, in the 1890s, his exploits were written up in the *Washington Post,* the *Chicago Herald,* the *Rochester Post Express*—newspapers from all over the land.

It is said that in his younger days he was affiliated with the Fenian Brotherhood, a secret society of hot-blooded Irishmen who invaded Canada from New York and Michigan in hope of capturing parts of it to trade for the freedom of their homeland. They were unsuccessful, of course, and lost much of their influence when American Archbishops Purcell and Spalding finally secured Rome's condemnation of the movement in 1870.

Jeremiah Crowley settled down after that, married a Sullivan, and started a family in Chicago. Five children were born in ten years, the oldest a son named Jerome. Jerome graduated from Chicago's Lake View High School in 1897 and went on to the University of Notre Dame. He stayed there only a year—long enough to publish articles on oratory in the *Notre Dame Scholastic,* to deliver a St. Patrick's Day oration (and win the year's award for elocution), and to sing with the University quartet for the likes of Archbishop John Ireland. He also won a medal for sculling across St. Joseph's Lake faster than anybody else. In 1898 he moved to Ann Arbor and the University of Michigan, carrying with him not only the medal he had won but also the memory of the young lady from St. Mary's College who had pinned it on him.

Jerome Crowley was a tall, handsome man who loved to act, loved to speak, loved to sing, loved to be with people. As a student he was "above the average," if we are to believe a letter of recommendation from his high school. Michigan was not the monastery that Notre Dame was in those days and it offered far more opportunities in theater. While his father was making news for his work in the opium traffic, the *Detroit Free Press* wrote of Jerome in 1900, "Mr. Crowley is one of the best tenors heard on college clubs in a long time. His voice is clear and high and he sings without effort." As Marcus Brutus Snap in the company, *A Night Off,* Jerome stole the show, according to another paper; at the curtain call the audience demanded that he deliver a speech.

Jerome's love of acting seems to have come from his father. Performing was fun for the elder Crowley and he thought it should remain just that for his son. Thus, when Jerome expressed an interest in pursuing his singing and acting professionally, his father took a dim view of the matter and insisted that he study the law. It was possible at that time to acquire a legal education during the undergraduate years, so when Jerome

Crowley graduated from Michigan in 1901, he was ready to begin a career not as a performer but as an attorney.

He returned to Chicago and in a few years formed a general practice firm with Rupert Barry, a friend from Michigan. Barry and Crowley, 100 West Monroe, concentrated on probate and corporate law, but the case they always bragged about was their successful defense in the 1920s of Shoeless Joe Jackson, a player for the Chicago "Black" Sox who was alleged to have taken gamblers' bribes.

On one occasion Jerome returned to South Bend for a meeting of the Knights of Columbus, a love of his father's to which he himself became dedicated. There, ten years after winning a medal for sculling, he again ran into Henrietta O'Brien.

Young Miss O'Brien happened to be the daughter of Patrick O'Brien, who had been born in Tipperary, Ireland, in 1837, and had come to South Bend by way of Philadelphia and Chicago. In the early 1870s Patrick had the good fortune of finding a way to make varnish dry faster, and in 1875 he translated his discovery into the O'Brien Electric Priming Company. (There was nothing "electric" about it; the word meant "quick.") Each of the three Studebaker brothers of South Bend put up $3,300 and Patrick $10,100 for the company's formal incorporation in 1878. In 1894 Patrick brought out the Studebakers for $36,000 and became the sole owner of what was then called the O'Brien Varnish Company. By that time O'Brien had built a large plant "way out in the country" at the corner of Washington and Johnson Streets in South Bend.

In the meantime, Patrick had married Matilda Byerley, daughter of one of South Bend's original families and together they had five sons and a daughter, Henrietta, who soon became the darling of her parents. By the time she pinned that medal on Jerome Crowley in 1898, the paint company was well established and the O'Briens were one of the leading families in South Bend.

Once they met a second time, the courtship of Henrietta O'Brien and Jerome Crowley proceeded with haste, and they were married on February 22, 1908. They settled in Chicago to be near Jerome's law practice and soon constructed a yellow-brick two-flat house on a small street near Lake Michigan, on the city's North Side. Each apartment in the building had four bedrooms, not counting the maid's room, and a bay window in the dining room from which one could see the lake at the end of the street. There was a long hallway leading to a spacious living room and then to a smaller room that became the Crowleys' "piano room," the most important in the house. The upstairs apartment had a balcony with an iron railing and the one beneath it had a front porch with a wicker swing big enough for three. Eventually the lake would be filled in to make way for an eight-lane expressway and high-rise apartments. But when Jerome and Henrietta moved into the downstairs flat of their new home, bringing with them a son named Jerry, the lake was still a few steps away. And so it was when a second son, Patrick, was born on September 23, 1911.

As Jerry and Pat grew up, they were almost inseparable and tried just about everything: ice skating, tennis, basketball, softball, BB guns, bicycle hikes to the forest preserves west of the city. There were fights, sometimes with rocks, with gangs from other streets. Pat once got a "knuckle sandwich" but he had the last laugh: his own teeth survived, but his assailant's knuckles became infected. There were Douglas Fairbanks movies, and the whole neighborhood would appear the next day with homemade swords and trash-can lids. On the next street was the alluring Robbins property, a whole block of open field leading down to the lake, dotted with two or three houses and a big barn full of old circus wagons. It was the perfect place for tree forts and dugouts. Once the Crowley boys set up a printing press in their basement, and on another occasion they built a sailboat. It was left at the beach at the end of the street, and many a time their mother would watch anxiously from the bay window as they took it out on the lake. And in the summer there were long, happy stays in South Bend with Grandmother O'Brien. Dad would commute to Chicago via the New York Central while his wife and children roamed Matilda's spacious home and enjoyed her hospitality.

The Crowleys were devout Catholics. Henrietta attended mass daily for much of her life and was active in organizations like the House of the Good Shepherd, the Big Sisters, the Cenacle, and the Christ Child Society. Her husband was a loyal Knight of Columbus. Their children were sent to the new parish school and became altar boys in the upper grades. Jerry was brighter in school than Pat, who was more carefree and often had to "stay after" to master a lesson. The Sisters of Mercy at St. Mary of the Lake were strict but good to the children, and the children were obedient. Practically all the Crowleys' friends were Catholic, and many of them were clergy who laughed, sang, drank, and discussed religion under the Crowley roof. In fact, on one of those visits to South Bend, young Patrick (he loved to tell the story later on) was bounced on the knee of Cardinal James Gibbons, very nearly *the* American Church in those days in the eyes of the American Republic.

Jerome Crowley was a Republican, but his brother George, all six feet seven inches of him, was an ardent and active Democrat. George often stopped at the Crowley house to discuss politics, though he and his brother rarely argued. Jerome once ran for probate judge but was swamped by Henry Horner, future governor of Illinois. He was also asked several times to run for mayor but declined because it would have meant contending with the likes of Anton Cermak. All of Jerome Crowley's professional life was spent in his small law office. He was counsel to the O'Brien Varnish Company from the time he married Henrietta, and became chairman of its board in 1943. In the words of his son Pat, he was "a decent lawyer, but not a great one." Other sources agree that he was far too fun-loving, too disorganized even, to be an outstanding attorney. Papers and mail were often strewn about his office. The firm got by, but not by much.

Jerome's heart was elsewhere. He poured himself into oratory (he was in great demand as a toastmaster), into the Knights of Columbus, into politics—into people. The Crowleys were part of an active, well-to-do circle of Irish Catholics who played bridge, went to parties and dances, golfed at the Edgewater Country Club, and vacationed at Biloxi, Mississippi, on the Gulf of Mexico.

After grammar school Jerry and Pat were sent to Loyola Academy, a Jesuit school on Chicago's lake front, just a few blocks north of the Sacred Heart Convent that Patty Caron would attend. Loyola in those days was a small, intimate school whose students came from prosperous Catholic families all over the city. Some rode the subway, some the city's buses, and some were wealthy enough to drive their own cars. The Jesuits ran a tight ship, but there were men like Father Brooks and Father Ed Dowling, for whom the students had great admiration. Father Dowling, in particular, had enormous influence on Pat's circle of friends—and on all the students at Loyola. His contact with them extended beyond school hours and even beyond the four years that students were at the academy. Even after he moved to St. Louis, Dowling kept alive a network of graduates whom he visited and counseled whenever he could. His meetings with the Loyola graduates who remained in Chicago led eventually to his association with the Cana Conference, a movement for married Catholics that blossomed in the late 1940s.

Academically, Jerry remained the better of the Crowleys at Loyola. Pat was two years younger than his brother but five inches taller, so he turned to football and fought his heart out playing tackle for the crack teams of coach Lenny Sachs, until in his senior year he was told he had "rheumatic heart fever." Pat was not exceptionally religious and certainly not a scholar. Those who knew him recall his friendly, outgoing manner, and his popularity with everybody. Ed Stephan, a classmate who became a friend for life, remembers Pat as a "normal kid of the age. None of his remarkable qualities surfaced at all, except his essential decency and goodness and *joie de vivre.*"

Tall, strong, and good-looking. Pat was a socialite—a "playboy," some say. By his senior year of high school, he and his crowd knew where the speakeasies were and how to get into them. In their chesterfield coats and spats and bowlers—and sometimes in tails—they were the adolescent dandies of the 1920s. They danced at places like the

Beachwalk of the Edgewater Beach Hotel, played golf and tennis at their parents' country clubs, and went to parties at summer homes at nearby Crystal Lake. Pat dated a lot but never had time to get serious about anyone. Too many parents were anxious for him to meet their daughters.

Jerry graduated from Loyola in 1927 and Pat in 1929. Both attended the University of Notre Dame. Jerry, clearly one of the volatile O'Briens in looks and personality, completed his studies in 1931 and Pat, the likeness of his father, finished in 1933. The depression hit the Crowleys while the boys were in college, just after the family returned from a glorious trip to Europe. Mr. Crowley lost money and his law firm came upon some lean years. But there was always the family paint company, and though its sales were cut by two-thirds, it managed to survive. As Jerry puts it, "We were never desperate or destitute or even close to it. We were able to continue to go to school and we ate well. I don't think it ever bothered my father much. He really didn't care that much about money, as long as there was enough to take care of people in a modest way. He was not a gambler. I mean, he wasn't the kind of fellow who would go into one venture after another trying to hit the jackpot."

Jerry went to work for the paint company after graduating from Notre Dame and served as its president from 1947 to 1975. He was just a few years short of seventy when he spoke, very softly, of Jerome and Henrietta, his mother and father. "They were quite perfectly married. Oh, she used to get sore at him once in a while. His idea of church or a train was, if you arrived there before it was time to take off, you were wasting your time. He was always at the edge. Her family, the O'Briens, were all perky, and they were all pretty quick-tempered. And their idea of getting to a train or getting to church was to get there fifteen or twenty minutes ahead of time. So that was the only real point of difference that they had. My mother worried, but eventually she was agreeable. I guess she learned she couldn't do anything about it."

Mrs. Crowley struck others as a strong woman, far more proper and meticulous, and certainly far more sober, than her husband. Yet his ebullience affected her, too, and at parties she would loosen up and do a little dance. She had been the queen of the O'Brien home and remained so among the Crowleys. Since there was always a maid, she never learned how to cook. "If you don't know how to cook," she would confide, "you never have to cook." Her two sons were all the more special because a third died in infancy. Jerry speaks of her as "a very kindly, loving, and affectionate soul. They were very easy on us, really. I think I would have been much better if I had had the clamps put on earlier and been more disciplined. I don't think it made any difference with Pat. He was just a natural. We were trusted and we were given a lot of freedom, and there was never any stern discipline of any kind. Once in a while, but mostly not. And they were extremely hospitable not only to their own friends but also to our friends. Tremendously hospitable."

The ease in the Crowley family, the warmth, the trust, the willingness to let the children *be,* came from the father. He hadn't begun life with an empty pail nor had he struggled to fill it again and again. He wasn't going anywhere nor striving to reach and hold onto something he had been deprived of. O. J. Caron started with nothing and attained wealth, but financially, Jerome Crowley ended up pretty much where he had started. Had he pursued the theater professionally, who knows?—he might have become a very different person. But, as it was, he lived all his married life in the same home and worked at the same profession in the same office. As counsel to the O'Brien Company he worked intimately with one of his sons, and he welcomed the other into his own law firm and eventually passed on its business. He was close to his offspring from beginning to end.

"He was always the same," said one who knew Jerome well. "I never saw him down. I never saw him cynical." The loves of his early life, music and people, were always with him. They kept him on an even keel, kept a smile on his face, delight in his eyes, cheer in his heart. Surely they sustained him as his wife lay dying in 1949 and as he neared his own death soon thereafter. On Henrietta's funeral card there appeared her "frequent meditation": "It is a blessed secret—living by the day. Anyone can carry his burden, however heavy, until nightfall. Anyone can do his work, however hard, for one day. God gives us nights to shut down the curtain of darkness on our little days. We cannot see beyond. Short horizons make life easier."

Live by the day: Henrietta preached it (as if to remind herself) but Jerome did it. It would be wrong to measure his life by the growth of business ventures (though he was a successful attorney) or by the accomplishments of his children (though they both achieved a great deal). His heritage was something else.

His only surviving son, father of ten and a grandfather as well, fought moistened eyes and a flood of memories to express it. "He was a noble soul, very easygoing. And he very, very rarely got mad at anybody. He wasn't too quick on making money—or wanting it, for that matter—but he was a noble heart. He liked helping people. He was really a prime target for a large number of people who wanted help or a job or free legal advice or a little money. He was a fairly busy lawyer, but I'm sure he did oodles of free work. People expected him to and he did. He had a lot of fun in him, too. He loved to give the ladies a big boost, a hug and kiss and all sorts of flowery compliments, and they all ate it up."

And Effie White, whose half-Black, half-Indian father had taught her that "everybody's people," that "the only difference between you and the next individual is just skin-deep," found one of her kind in Mr. Crowley. She met him after Mrs. Crowley died and Mr. Crowley had moved in with his two aging sisters. She was their maid and has been the maid, and sometimes the second mother, of three generations of his progeny. "He was the sweetest thing God ever let live. He was beautiful. Just beautiful. I remember when I was working for him, he would always follow me to the elevator and give me an extra dollar for to buy my cigarettes and shake my hand. And it wasn't just shake and turn loose, it was a handshake of love. You could feel it. You could feel the love that went with it. He'd say, 'Here's a little something extra, Effie, for you to buy your cigarettes.' And I'd say, 'Thank you, Mr. Crowley.' And he'd say, 'Good-bye, be careful going home.'"

And a granddaughter, speaking softly in the refectory of a Benedictine convent, remembered the fun of days at Wrigley Field (even if the Cubs did lose), the thrill of long trips to see the O'Briens in Detroit, and always, the joy of the piano room, Grandmother playing, Granddaddy leading the chorus. Grandmother was "strict," "very proper," and "got upset very easily." "At least," she said, "those are the things you remember. She was a very happy person, but she was also very demanding. But Granddaddy was not like that at all. He was a very peaceful kind of person. My cousin and I loved him. We were just very close to him."

Surely Jerome Crowley knew trouble, difficulty, pain, and disappointment in that steady life of his; but when they came, he must have kept them to himself. For in the minds of those who came after him he is welcoming guests, singing "Easter Parade," kissing the ladies, offering the children candy from that special blue dish. His son Pat, who was always very close to him, who felt his support throughout his life, often said, "The apple doesn't fall far from the tree."

Honeymoon, 1937.

CHAPTER FOUR
PAT AND PATTY

1940—the beginning of the poker club.

With daughter Patsy in 1946.

Only an older generation of American Catholics knows how boring a *Tre Ore* can be—or, for that matter, what a *Tre Ore* is. Not too long ago, it seems, good Catholics would fast on the morning of Good Friday and then gather from noon until three o'clock to commemorate the last words of Jesus on the cross. Since the last words were few, most of the three hours *(tre ore)* were filled with sermons, and they had to be digested on an empty stomach. It was quite natural, then, that as the service droned on, the eyes of young ladies who were present—no matter how "proper" they were—would search out whatever young men the church held at that odd time of day.

Patty Caron was home from Trinity College for Easter vacation in 1934 and, like any good Catholic, visited a string of churches on Holy Thursday and attended the *Tre Ore* on Good Friday. She was with her mother on Friday, so naturally the two arrived early at Holy Name Cathedral and assured themselves of a seat. It didn't take her long to notice two handsome late arrivals who, finding all the pews filled, took turns disappearing into the center box of a confessional to rest in the only seat available. Theirs was a three-hour act—in and out, in and out—not easily forgotten.

Two days later when Patty accompanied a date to a party, she was introduced to one of the performers. "I saw you in church," she said, and sat down to a game of poker. Pat Crowley was struck by Patricia Caron and immediately dealt her in. The fact that the cards went his way the rest of the night only strengthened the impression she made.

The next day Pat tried desperately to reach her. Since he couldn't remember her exact name, he opened a phone book and tried a dozen that seemed close. Unsuccessful, he decided to tweak the nose of diplomacy and call her escort of the night before. He got what he was after, but Patty already had returned to Trinity.

At the time, she was finishing her sophomore year. Trinity would prove to be a good influence on her, another case of not knowing anybody and having to make her own way. She was neither a top student nor a class leader, nor was she contemplating anything but marriage for the future. But she did stumble into a course taught by Monsignor John A. Ryan, a social ethician from nearby Catholic University and author of books like *The Living Wage* and *Distributive Justice*. Still active in his sixties, Ryan was director of the Social Action Department of the National Catholic Welfare Conference and the country's principal Catholic spokesman for the social reforms of Roosevelt's New Deal. In two years he would publicly debate Father Charles Coughlin, the controversial and influential "radio priest" from Royal Oak, Michigan.

Patty had no idea who Ryan was. "I took his course because everyone said it was easy. Everybody used to write all their letters home in his course, because he would read out of his books. But a couple of us sat up in front and found, if we got him out of the book, he was fascinating. We were learning something we had never heard about before." *Rerum Novarum, Quadragesimo Anno,* minimum-wage legislation, old-age insurance, labor unions (anathema to O. J. Caron): there was a Catholic social doctrine that went back more than fifty years. When Ryan and Patty happened to take the same train to Chicago at Christmastime and he bought her dinner, his influence was set. "I didn't realize what was happening to me then, but now I know," she says.

Patty had dated little before she met Pat and then only under the close supervision of her mother. "I was brought up to be very strict and I would be very careful when I dated—especially about kissing. Sacred Heart didn't help." Even during her junior year in the foreigners' program at the Sorbonne in Paris, when she dated a Yugoslav and a Frenchman, she was carefully chaperoned.

Pat, on the other hand, had taken out a number of girls but had never been so grievously smitten on a first meeting. He had finished at Notre Dame the year before, having led the same affable but undistinguished life he did at Loyola Academy. An average student, he was not particularly involved in class politics (such as they were in those days) or athletics, nor was he exceptionally religious. He belonged to the local chapter of the Knights of Columbus, as had his father and grandfather before him. He attended meetings of the Notre Dame Chicago Club and played tennis and golf. He was a good conformist who kept the rules, except for playing the horses once in a while, and he was very congenial. Everybody liked Pat Crowley.

Notre Dame during his stay was nearly as monastic as Pat's father had found it at the turn of the century. In the classroom there was an emphasis on apologetics, and in the strictly run residence halls an insistence on religious duties. Receive daily communion (even if you missed most of mass), say the rosary, go to devotions, defend the Faith. The religious atmosphere on campus was symbolized by Father (later Cardinal) John O'Hara, the prefect of religion. O'Hara wrote and mimeographed a daily religious bulletin that was slipped under the door of every student's room before the rising bell sounded. He knew everyone in the school by name and kept track of those who were absent from mass. "I haven't seen you at the rail in a week," he often announced to startled delinquents he met on campus. The prowess of his memory became legendary.

In the dormitories, students argued philosophy, had late-night bull sessions about social issues, played penny-ante poker, and shot craps. The Crowley brothers and friends Ed Stephan and Bill Dreux escaped the tight discipline with a monthly trip to Chicago, ninety miles to the northwest. Chicago was safe from the good fathers on campus, and liquor and beer were accessible, Prohibition or not. Pat drank as much as everybody else, but he always got mellow, never belligerent. Stephan, who often stayed with the Crowley family on weekends in Chicago, remembers Saturday nights that ended at five the next morning. A few hours later Mrs. Crowley would knock on the boys' bedroom door to wake them in time for church.

Football weekends were the major events of the year. Students brought dates from their hometowns and lodged them at the Oliver Hotel. Girl friends of the Crowleys enjoyed the hospitality of the South Bend O'Briens. For two years Pat never missed a Saturday on which the Fighting Irish of Coach Knute Rockne took the field against their outmanned foes. But in 1931 Rockne was killed in an airplane crash, and the campus closed down and plunged into mourning.

By Pat's junior year the depression was casting another pall on student life. Since spending allowances from home were cut, Pat and his friends developed an elaborate lending system. Anyone who received a check split it on the spot and everyone went to a movie, each keeping track of who owed whom how much. But by the time of the senior ball even checks from home were of no help because local banks would not cash them. Franklin Roosevelt took office in January of Pat's senior year, and throughout the ensuing months students hovered around the radio listening to the beginnings of the New Deal. "There is nothing to fear but fear itself," Roosevelt said, but Ed Stephan admits "we were all pretty scared." Many plans for law or medical school had to be postponed. Students hoped for nothing more than to find a job.

The influence of John Ryan was felt at Notre Dame as it was at Trinity and other Catholic colleges across the country. In his senior year, as Roosevelt unfolded his plans, Pat took a course in Distributive Justice, in which the text was Ryan's book of the same name. In the space of four months Pat was exposed to the same Catholic social tradition that Patty would meet a year later, and it made the same positive impression upon him. (His friend Ed Stephan argued that "distributive justice" meant that drinkers of Cokes should not have to kick in as much as drinkers of liquor when the tabs were paid in Chicago's speakeasies. But Stephan—and distributive justice—always lost out to Pat Crowley.)

Pat survived a near-failure in a Natural Theology course and graduated in June, 1933. The fieldhouse with its dirt floor was hot and steamy on commencement day, and so was the oratory. For political reflection there was Al Smith, defeated four-and-a-half years previously as the country's first Catholic candidate for president, and Father Coughlin, still taking credit for dumping Hoover and putting Roosevelt in office. (In a few years Coughlin would turn against Roosevelt, become anti-Semitic, and draw Ryan's ire.) For entertainment there was the renowned Irish tenor, John McCormick.

It was only natural that Pat had begun to think in his senior year of entering the law. His father had a practice the sons could enter; his older brother chose the paint company instead. Apparently Mr. Crowley planned to send Pat to Harvard for his legal education but was unable to because of the depression. So friends got a job for Pat at Chicago Title and Trust Company, and in the fall he started evening classes at Loyola University's School of Law. Although the work at Chicago Title and Trust was dull, Pat gained there what he could not have at Harvard: a knowledge of how the city worked as well as a host of political contacts that would serve him well for the rest of his life. Chicago's bureaucracy was frustrating, but he discovered someone on the sixth floor of the County Building who would give a straight answer and get things done. His name was Richard Daley.

Pat was in the middle of his second semester of law school that particular Good Friday when he arrived late for the *Tre Ore*. Though Patty found him quite resistible at first, he pursued her relentlessly. He played tennis with her when she returned to Chicago for the summer and wrote her faithfully during her junior year in Europe, even though she responded sporadically. In her senior year at Trinity they dated when she came home for Christmas, and he made several trips East, one of them by air (a novelty in 1936) for her senior prom. Once, at a party in New York's Plaza Hotel, he whispered to Ed Stephan, "I think something is happening to me." Ed cracked, "Do you need medication?"

By that time something was happening to Patty, too. "Still," she says, "I was influenced by my mother, who didn't think you should get married right away after school. She wanted me to have a good time. So the year after I got out of school I went to Florida and visited some friends. I didn't do anything."

When Patty returned from Florida, it was a busy young man who came to her house for warmed-over dinners and took her to mass at St. Peter's and breakfast at Henrici's every Tuesday morning. Pat often accompanied his mother to Tuesday evening novenas and Patty started to go along, too. "I was comfortable with him and I think that was the beginning of it. I don't know whether I really was in love with him until he started coming every night to the house and we got to know each other." But Patty's mother and father were dead set against her marrying "a lazy Irishman." I cried so many nights because they didn't think I should marry him. It was my mother mostly. Once again she was trying to protect me."

Pat's family was far less cautious about Patty. There was an ease in the Crowley home that was new to her. There was singing, which she had never known as a child; and guests were welcomed simply because they were guests, not business contacts to be entertained. Mr. Crowley was his delightful, buoyant self, but "I remember always worrying that I wasn't pleasing Mrs. Crowley, that I wouldn't be just what she thought I should be. She really loved Pat."

O. J. broke the ice on the Caron side when he said he would permit Patty's engagement on the condition that Pat was making fifty dollars a week—the amount O. J. had been earning when he proposed to his own wife twenty-five years before. Marvelous, thought Pat, that's what I *am* making (well, who would call me a liar for a measly five bucks?). Marietta made Pat promise never to enter politics, and the wedding was on.

On April 24, 1937, the twenty-fifth wedding anniversary of O. J. and Marietta Caron, Pat and Patty had their engagement party. "One of the most beautiful parties I ever had. Garlands of gardenias," her mother wrote in her diary.

Before the wedding Pat and Patty had lunch with Father Dowling and received private "marriage instruction," as counseling was called in those days. A short time later, in the course of a long conversation the night before Ed Stephan's wedding, he pleaded with Ed "to teach me the ropes quickly." Having learned what he could about marriage, Pat was ready when his own time came.

"They were married October 16, 1937," said Mrs. Caron's notes. "A beautiful wedding. The night before their wedding Dad told Patty she could always come home if she were unhappy, but I said no. If she wanted to change her mind that night, I would welcome her home, but after the ceremony it was between Pat and her."

By all accounts the Caron-Crowley wedding at Mount Carmel Church was as beautiful as Mrs. Caron remembered. It was fun, too, with plenty of young people to complement the friends and relatives of the parents. Fifteen of Patty's friends from faraway Trinity attended. Puddy Giblin, her roommate in Europe, met Pat's brother Jerry and eventually married him. The dancing continued long after the couple set off by train for California, where they were to catch a boat for Honolulu. (Even though Mrs. Crowley paid for the honeymoon, it was Mrs. Caron who thought it should take place in Hawaii. Apparently not everything was to be "between Pat and her.") A boat strike on the West Coast forced a change in plans, however, and Pat and Patty had to choose between Alaska and the Panama Canal. They weren't dressed for Alaska, so they chose the Canal and had a wonderful cruise to New York. Mother Caron was disappointed—the Canal, after all, was not Hawaii—but in time she got over it.

So Pat and Patty settled down to a marriage indistinguishable from others of that time and place. They did what their friends did. He went to work and she stayed home. They went to church. They went to cocktail parties where all the men stood in one corner and talked baseball and all the women stood in another and talked babies. For a year they were parents to Patty's teenage sister Joan, who wanted to stay in Chicago and finish at Sacred Heart when the Carons moved to Rochelle. Pat failed the bar exam the first time around but had better luck six months later. ("I think I prayed the whole day that he would pass," Patty says of the traumatic trip to Springfield.) The highlights of their life, though, were football weekends at Notre Dame, drinks before the game and cocktail parties after, nights spent with the O'Briens, one of *the* families of South Bend. "I knew that mother would be impressed with his friends down there, and she was. His aunt lived in one of the biggest houses in South Bend and gave fancy parties with maids passing food and drinks around. Mother was very impressed with all that, and that made me feel good because I wanted her to be impressed with Pat and his family." Eventually, Mrs. Caron changed her mind about the Irish. In the years to come nearly all her friends were made, in one way or another, through the hospitality of the Crowleys.

After passing the bar Pat moved into his father's law office. Business was in a slump at the time, but Pat revived it when a friend asked him to manage a large estate. Then Bob Folonie died, leaving the Caron Spinning Company without legal counsel. Folonie was one of the original founders of the company and a lifelong friend of O. J. and Marietta—Patty's godfather, in fact. His absence was deeply felt. Out of desperation more than anything else, the Carons turned to Pat; and, though he was barely out of law school, he performed superbly. He offered sound advice and had a wellspring of patience and tact, every drop of which was needed in dealing with the Carons.

Sometime later, a friend by the name of Charles Caestecker asked Pat to do the legal work for a plastics company begun in Caestecker's garage. His American Molded Products account was another that put the Crowleys' law firm back on its feet after the depression. When Pat began to take an active role in the O'Brien Varnish Company, the outlines of his lifetime career as a business lawyer were set. Most of his work would be as an officer in and counsel to the Caron and O'Brien companies. While he never managed them on a day-to-day basis, as the confidante, the idea man, the judge of prospective moves, he was in constant contact with the presidents of both. And his business sense proved to be uncanny.

The first of the Crowley children, Patricia Ann, was born on the thirteenth of May, 1939, and called Patsy. For four years she was the only child. There was a miscarriage, an infant death, and then in 1943 Mary Ann was born. Patrick, their first son, came in 1944. Patsy was taken everywhere by her mother—even to breakfast in the Pump Room of the Drake Hotel—and was lucky enough to join her cousin Jerome for overnight visits at the home of Grandmother and Granddaddy Crowley and to stay with the Carons in Rochelle. Mary Ann was often sick as an infant and required the attention of a nurse, but Patrick, a chubby, healthy boy, was little trouble. Before the younger two arrived, the Crowleys had done what "everybody did" and moved to the suburbs. With the help of a gift from Pat's mother, they built a beautiful home at 2304 Elmwood in Wilmette. There they formed a "stork club" and later a "poker club" with friends of long standing. The stork brought plenty of babies but the group rarely played poker.

A month after the move to Wilmette and shortly after the Crowleys' infant daughter died, Japan attacked Pearl Harbor. Pat and Patty were spared what followed. Pat's draft status was ambiguous, but he had enough children to exempt him from service. Draft boards insisted, however, that those who did not fight participate somehow in the war effort, so Pat took a job in 1942 with the estate and property division of the Alien Property Custodian, the government agency that seized large German and Japanese companies in this country. On occasion his legal work for the APC brought him in contact with Japanese-Americans in detention camps, and he was disturbed by what he saw. But the horror of World War II came no closer.

In fact, the decade before the war—hard times for many Americans—was a pleasant episode in the lives of Pat and Patty. The Carons and the Crowleys never saw the family businesses go under, never had to let the maids go, and saw only one son leave for war (he returned safely). Pat and Patty went away to college, traveled in Europe, met, married, honeymooned, had children, and moved to the suburbs. Pat stepped into his father's office and succeeded there. He and his wife had a great many friends and a set, albeit strict, view of life. If anyone had told them the world they lived in, for all its trips to Europe and journeys through the Canal, was a narrow one, they would not have comprehended.

They were living the Good Life, excused from the sorrow of the times. But their sense of being spared began to instill a disquietude. "As the headlines became more and more tragic," Pat wrote of that period, "the hunger to do something positive and permanent gnawed deeper inside—though perhaps it didn't show much outside."

Pat and Patty Crowley were ready for an idea.

Important figures in Chicago's "Catholic Action" of the 1940s: Pat and Patty with Monsignor Reynold Hillenbrand and Cardinal Samuel Stritch.

CHAPTER FIVE
JOSEPH CARDIJN: FROM BELGIUM TO WILMETTE

Canon Joseph Cardijn.

Pat, Father Gerard Weber, chaplain of the first women's group, and Chicagoan Peter Fitzpatrick.

In 1903, when Joseph Cardijn turned twenty-one, he saw his father die and realized he had incurred a debt. The man he had lost had spared him the fate of classmates who stepped from grammar school into the horrible factories of Belgium. It was not because the Cardijns had wealth or connections. It was rather that the father of the family worked himself excessively, literally to death, so his son could pursue his dream of entering the seminary and becoming a priest. Even during his sheltered seminary years Cardijn could not put his former schoolmates, and all of their generation, out of his mind. "During my seminary holidays we used to talk about them at home every day, and I used to see groups of them going past morning and evening on their way to work." They were still children, "forsaken, neglected and demoralized," when they began to work. His father's years as a caretaker and coal merchant exempted him from that. "I vowed at his deathbed to consecrate myself to the salvation of working youth and the working class. This vow became the guiding motive of my life."[1]

After his father's death, Cardijn toured the industrial regions of his country and took a hard look at the conditions surrounding these young workers. He devoured what he could find of Church teaching on the worker: Ozanam in France, von Ketteler in Germany, Gibbons in the United States, Manning in England, and Leo XIII's *Rerum Novarum*, promulgated when Cardijn was nine years old. Catholics were leaving the Church because it looked the other way (as Marxism did not) in the face of unspeakable oppression in the factories. The children to whom Cardijn taught catechism after his ordination quickly lost interest in religion after a few days in the worker environment. They never came back.

What was happening? Cardijn persuaded a group of former students to return every week and report on their experiences in the factories. They were workers; he was not. They could see with the eyes of workers what he was bound to miss. Simply observe, he said, and realize (perhaps for the first time) what is going on. After a while Cardijn asked his catechists to judge what they were seeing in light of Christian principles. The group responded and soon began to plan initiatives to better their situation. Now act, he counseled, or else you will become mired in endless discussion. Observe-Judge-Act: a formula straight from Aquinas, simple, direct, effective. The so-called "Inquiry Method" was born.

Before long Cardijn organized three thousand seamstresses who had been powerless against the abuses of their *patrons*. During World War I the Germans jailed him for his unionist activities. There he perfected his thinking on technique: small cells of workers would follow the Inquiry Method and eventually become leaders in their factories. Oddly enough, it was patterned after the method of the communists, whom

Cardijn regarded as a serious threat to his students. After the war, Cardijn's *Jeunesse Ouvriére Chrétienne*—Working Christian Youth—grew in strength and spread rapdily. In English the movement came to be known as YCW—Young Christian Workers—or as the Jocists, after the French acronym JOC.

Struggling to get past officials in the Roman Curia, Canon Cardijn finally brought his ideas to Pius XI in 1925. The pope welcomed them and addressed letters to the national hierarchies advocating use of the Cardijn technique. His definition of Catholic Action as "the participation of the laity in the apostolic mission of the hierarchy" and his issuance of the labor encyclical *Quadragesimo Anno* in 1931 created the climate for YCW's diffusion throughout the globe. How large it grew is difficult to measure, but in 1957 thirty thousand workers from eighty-seven countries on five continents gathered in St. Peter's Square in Rome. It was estimated, perhaps generously, that they represented more than two million others.

Cardijn, a short, intense, highly disciplined man, never thought of himself as a teacher, a theologian, or a writer. He was, in his own words, a "great traveler," "a man of action always on the move, always searching and enquiring."[2] Though he stressed action, his greatest contribution was an *idea*, derived from a practical necessity, spreading wherever the need existed. At the time his young worker friends began to go where he could not, to see and do what he could not, the laity in the Catholic Church did little else but "pay and pray." Cardijn's idea was radical: lay men and women were "apostles" no less than priests. The mass offered by the clergy was to be prolonged by the laity "on all those altars of secular life: the worktable, the loom, the lathe, the joiner's bench, the typist's desk."[3] If the laity were workers, their apostolate would be to workers. If farmers, they were responsible for farmers; if students, for other students (and so there developed in France the *Jeunesse Étudiante Chrétienne,* Young Christian Students). Like was to minister to like—no one else could—and that made the laity indispensable.

One of those reached by the idea was Louis Putz, a German Holy Cross seminarian studying in Paris in the midthirties. Putz spent one year before and three years after ordination working in the industrial ring surrounding Paris—in the "red zone," as it was called because of the substantial communist presence among its workers. "In Paris in 1936," Putz relates, "you had to be a communist to amount to anything. You couldn't get any social security or social welfare at all if you were not a communist." For four years he used Cardijn's Inquiry Method to organize teenage workers into *Jeunesse Ouvriére Chrétienne.* Then, a German citizen living in France, he was forced to leave by the outbreak of the Second World War.

Putz emigrated to the United States and was given a position at his congregation's University of Notre Dame. He found there was already talk of Cardijn in the Midwest—thanks to two men who had arrived in the States the year before. An Australian named Paul McGuire had given a number of lectures, two of them at Notre Dame, and had stimulated the formation of YCW groups in San Francisco and Toledo, though both were to prove unsuccessful. Father Donald Kanaly, returning to this country after studies at Belgium's Louvain University, had addressed a number of priests in the Chicago area and established a YCW in Oklahoma. But, according to Putz, neither McGuire nor Kanaly had worked as intimately as he with the Cardijn method (they had, in fact, only observed it), so Putz quickly became a source of practical expertise.

Putz first organized a handful of Notre Dame graduate students moved by a description of his activities in France. Anxious to do something but not knowing what or how (graduate courses in apologetics never got around to that), they readily formed a cell called Catholic Action Students. It was a vigorous group. In May of 1940 they published the first issue of a monthly, the *Catholic Action Apostle*, and sent it to other college groups in the Midwest. Then they created new services on campus: a book exchange to undercut secondhand book dealers who made huge profits off students, a press to enable students to print materials for their organizations without paying exorbitant prices in town, a Mardi Gras to raise money for European students. When the University's administration told them there were no Negroes on campus because students from the South were opposed to it, they took a survey that proved otherwise. The following fall Notre Dame enrolled its first black student. Later the Catholic Action students sponsored retreats in residence halls and a series of lectures on marriage for graduating seniors. The lectures were delivered by laity as well as by clergy, something unusual in those days. In time the *Catholic Action Apostle* became *Concord*, which grew eventually into Fides Publishing Company.

In 1941 Father Putz was invited by Monsignor Reynold Hillenbrand to speak to a group of his deacons at Chicago's archdiocesan seminary in Mundelein, Illinois. Hillenbrand, already acquainted with Jocist thinking through Father Kanaly, had organized a cell of students at Senn High School in 1939 (a leader in that cell was George "Red" Sullivan, who later became the first national president of YCW) and was, according to writers Daniel Callahan and Andrew Greeley, *the* charismatic figure in the ferment that characterized Chicago's Catholicism in the 1930s.[4] The Midwest in that era witnessed numerous experiments in Catholic action, far more than were taking place in other parts of the country. Catholic liberals there were discovering the social teachings of the Church with the same fervor that non-Catholics were turning to the pages of Karl Marx. Chicago's Bishop Bernard Sheil was championing the causes of labor unions and community organizations, while the Archdiocesan paper, *The New World*, was taking liberal positions on political and social questions. Father Daniel Cantwell and others were about to form the Catholic Interracial Council and the Catholic Labor Alliance. A Jesuit by the name of Michael Carrabine created the Chicago Inter-Student Catholic Action (CISCA), and from it sprang such individuals as Edward Marciniak, who went on to edit *Work* and direct the Chicago Commission on Human Relations, John Cogley and James O'Gara, who both became editors of *Commonweal*, and Father John Egan, a leader in many of the Catholic Action organizations that flourished in Chicago after World War II. It was Marciniak, Cogley, and O'Gara who introduced to Chicago Dorothy Day's Catholic Worker Movement, begun in New York in 1933.

Hillenbrand was appointed rector of St. Mary of the Lake Seminary by Cardinal Mundelein in 1935. He was in his early thirties at the time, but already a dedicated liturgist thoroughly familiar with the social encyclicals. The young men trained under him, *all* of Chicago's future priests, were presented with the same vision that guided Cardijn in Belgium: a community of Christians formed through worship, inspired by the Church's social teachings, goes forth into the world to correct social evils and returns periodically to be refreshed by the liturgy. There were numerous meetings, conferences, seminars, study weeks, and training programs while Hillenbrand was at Mundelein, the most extensive being two monthlong sessions in the summers of 1938 and 1939 that brought together leaders of Catholic action groups and prominent union officials. Father Putz was invited to one of Hillenbrand's meetings, and even though Hillenbrand fell asleep during his presentation (something that amuses Putz to this day), the details of Observe-Judge-Act made the desired impression on his deacons.

One of those deacons had a lay friend by the name of Paul Hazard. Hazard had been a seminarian himself but left in 1933 for reasons of health (a bad back, according to Pat Crowley, who never failed to add that Hazard managed somehow to father eight children). The Jocists dealt with workers and students, the deacon informed Hazard, but what about businessmen, professionals? Hazard, an insurance salesman, pondered that question before springing it one night early in 1943 on another friend named Frank Crowe. "We were talking about the hopelessness of the future and I mentioned this idea of starting a cell for businessmen as a little something we could do. And Crowe thought it was a great idea. I told him I thought it was crazy, but he thought he would like to try it. So we ended up killing a case of beer and deciding that we would try to get some of our friends. The first guy we got was Pat Crowley."

Hazard's parents had known the elder Crowleys for some time, though Paul had never met Pat until he sold him an insurance policy. When he returned to sell Catholic Action, he found his customer had already been primed by Chick Sheedy, a college friend and now a priest at Notre Dame. Within a few weeks six men, all in their thirties and all married, were meeting with a chaplain in Pat's office in downtown Chicago—the only office, it seems, where the boss (in this case Pat's father) would allow them to get together after hours. Soon Father Putz was meeting with them and explaining the Jocist technique, and Monsignor Hillenbrand was instructing them in the liturgy. Shortly afterward, too, in May, 1943, a remarkable document was issued from Rome.

To hear Pat embellish the story years later, it seemed that Pius XII learned of these six guys meeting in a little joint on Monroe Street and issue *Mystici Corporis Christi* to clear up some of the problems occurring in their discussions. It is true that the timing of the encyclical *was* uncanny. Here was Monsignor Hillenbrand telling a handful of businessmen, "Christ shares His work with you. You are the hands of Christ, in the most noble sense; where you work, Christ works. You are the feet of Christ in the most noble sense; wherever you go, Christ goes. You are the heart of Christ; wherever you go, the love of Christ is found because you love people. You are the lips of Christ; whatever you articulate, you are articulating for Christ." And after his exhortation came an encyclical from Rome building on Paul's first letter to the Corinthians, expressing identical sentiments. Pat's story continued: "We learned that we had a role to play in the Church, that we *were* the Church. This was back in 1943. I had gone to Notre Dame, but they didn't know about it when I was there. Nobody else knew about it, but we did and the Pope did. So he wrote about our group."

Some group. Despite the effort of chaplain Julian Marhoeffer, it stumbled along, recruiting new members while losing old ones, suffering spotty attendance at meetings. It had nothing specific to work on. "We tried to find out what common interests existed in the group, and there really weren't any," Pat recollected. "There were all kinds of different jobs: lawyers, insurance salesmen—others who worked for a living. One night a guy came along and said, 'Well, everybody in the group is married.' Now that wasn't very remarkable, because if you weren't married in 1943, you weren't home. But we decided anyhow that we'd straighten out marriage and then move on to something serious."

The group's first marriage inquiry concerned the soaring divorce rate in Chicago and its first action was the creation of a network of "experts"—doctors, lawyers, accountants, members of Alcoholics Anonymous—who made themselves available, through the Chancery Office, to anyone considering divorce. Some of the group attended a "Family Renewal Day" at Sacred Heart Convent in suburban Lake Forest. Directed by John Delaney, a Jesuit from New York, the day proved to be exhilarating. Never had the Church spoken to any of them about marriage. Their next step was clear: get some priests and run our own family renewal. One of the first contacted was Father Edward Dowling, the Jesuit who had taught at Loyola Academy and given private marriage instructions to his favorite alumni. Father Dowling came up from St. Louis, sat in on a discussion, found its enthusiasm contagious, and returned home with the idea of a "Cana Conference." It blossomed into a movement which grew beyond anyone's expectation in St. Louis, Chicago, and eventually throughout the nation.

So the men's Catholic Action group struck gold by directing its efforts to the family. By October, 1946, they were confident enough to speak of themselves as a "federation" and to bring out the first issue of *Act*, a four-page "Quarterly of Adult Catholic Action." The original cell of six was now six cells scattered around Chicago, fifty men bringing Cardijn's Inquiry Method to problems of marriage and the family.

"Absolutely ridiculous," Patty Crowley said years later. "The men were never home and they were talking about marriage." She resented those weekly meetings. "We would go to a party and Pat would have a few martinis and he'd talk about this Mystical Body and it was always so funny. But I didn't like it because I wasn't part of it." Her first encounter with the revered Monsignor Hillenbrand didn't help. Driving home from a party, Pat suddenly slammed on the brakes. " 'There's Monsignor,' he said, like there was a god right there on the street corner. I thought I was going to meet this great, great guy and be very impressed. So Monsignor got in the car, we drove him up to Winnetka, and he didn't say one word all the way home. Pat got out, and I said, 'Oh, that's your guy, is it? He's very scintillating.' "

It wasn't because of Monsignor's shyness with women, of course, that the wives of the men in the Catholic Action Federation were becoming irritated. Nor was Pat's interpretation, told over the years for the amusement of audience after audience, entirely accurate: "Our wives were getting a little worried. We were getting fairly holy and talking, you know, about how Saint Bernard convinced his brother to leave his wife and ten children and become a monk." No, the women were simply getting tired of seeing their husbands coming home in a state of euphoria and excluding them from whatever it was that made them so high. So the wives formed a cell of their own with Father Gerard Weber as chaplain. Patty refused to join because meeting apart from the men made no sense to her. In time, though, she relented and discovered, like all the others, an unimagined source of stimulation: adult women talking to each other for the first time in their lives about something serious. The situation did not lack irony. "The women, instead of talking about children, were talking about social issues—which they didn't know anything about—and the men, instead of talking about social issues, were talking about children—which they didn't know anything about." The women met once a week with a chaplain (in those days you never considered doing otherwise), discussed the Scriptures (something new for Catholic laity), and studied, say, a *Commonweal* article on work or prejudice. Before that, "lay people never expressed themselves religious-wise. They would always turn to the priest and say, is that correct?" But now the chaplains remained silent and many learned a great deal. Their only contribution never varied: *you* are the laity, *you* have a role to play, *you* can do what we cannot.

One of the women's inquiries resulted in a hundred packages of food and clothing being shipped to European refugees, another to a play about prejudice put on by their children (it raised fifty dollars for Friendship House, a storefront meetinghouse for blacks and whites). Someone observed that her sister was getting married without benefit of the Cana-type instructions they themselves had received. The women immediately formulated the action of running a day for engaged couples. Pre-Cana, they called it. "Another girl and I went around to about ten parishes, trying to get the names of newly married or engaged couples so we could invite them to this first Pre-Cana. Most of the priests threw us out of the rectory. I mean, a couple of women coming to get names! But some did listen, though they thought it was a big joke. How could anybody tell people about marriage? But we got enough interest so that we had about twenty couples. Father Dowling gave that one and it was a great success." It was such a success that many similar days were organized in the future. A companion movement to Cana was off and running.

Men and women in the Catholic Action cells still met separately, however, even though the activities of the women were being written up in *Act*. The men were becoming puzzled (and pleasantly surprised) when their wives started to talk about bills before Congress instead of babies. A visiting YCW priest from England, Father John Fitzsimons, thought their cell meetings marvelous but wondered out loud why the separate groups didn't meet together. "To meet together was unheard of then," Patty remembers. Never at Church, or, indeed, on any social occasion did men and women talk together, much less about something serious. Though some chaplains threatened to resign if the groups came together, Patty "loved the idea because then I could go to meetings with Pat. So Pat and I started a group in St. Joseph parish and somebody else started one in another parish. We had a monsignor who was a gruff old German and we asked him to give us a chaplain. He said, 'Well, it won't work but you can try.' So we started the couples' group. We all realized how we enjoyed it, how we got to know other couples in a different way. It was very interesting: the women did all of the talking."

So changes were taking place, subtle changes in the role of women, in the role of the laity, for the simple reason that the time was right and the next step natural. In Paris, in 1946, the red-zone workers whom Father Putz had known as teenagers, married now, organized themselves into the *Mouvement Populaire de Famille*. In the aftermath of the war they wanted to continue their Jocist activities—but only *as families*. A year later Catholic Action groups in South Bend and Chicago decided to meet as couples and concentrate on family life. (Even during the war, Burnie Bauer, one of Putz's original Catholic Action students, tried with his wife Helene to develop a couples' group in South Bend. But the war called most of the men and the group failed.) By the end of 1948, *Act* reported, there were twenty cities in the United States that had cells of Catholic men and women working on the "family apostolate." Undoubtedly there were many more that escaped *Act's* notice.

In Chicago a new structure was created to formalize the momentum toward couples' groups. The federation of "Catholic Action" was renamed "Christian Family Action"—"Christian" to allow for a broader base of membership in the future and to accommodate couples in "mixed" marriages, "Family" to capture an emphasis that was now unstoppable. CFA, *Act* enthused early in 1949, "expects to leaven the whole mass of American family life." The Chicago federation had three divisions, one each for men's and women's groups and one for couples' groups, now in the majority. Recruiting for new "sections," as cells were renamed, had been done through Cana Conferences and personal friendships. As 1949 opened there were five hundred people in the federation. Its president was Pat Crowley.

Chicago's CFA was fortunate to have the support of Cardinal Stritch almost from the beginning. Though he removed Hillenbrand from the seminary in 1944 and replaced him with a man who shared none of his fervor for social action, the action was a blessing in disguise: Hillenbrand became pastor at Sacred Heart in Hubbard Woods, where he was directly available to the movement. Stritch's appointment of Father John Egan as chaplain of Cana and Pre-Cana and Father William Quinn as chaplain of Catholic Action—both made in 1946 at the request of the federations—was felicitous as far as the Crowleys and their fellow couples were concerned. They received an additional vote of confidence when they were asked by the archdiocese to represent Chicago at a national meeting of family life directors in 1947. (Their presence created an uproar among participants from other dioceses, who were used to seeing only Roman collars.) The climate in Chicago was nurturant, and would be so for another two decades.

But there was more to the growth of these Catholic Action efforts than a supportive prelate. The men and women of whom I write discovered by trial and error that whenever their technique, begun in the factories of Belgium, was directed at the family, minds and hearts were stirred, their own as well as others'. Until they hit that bullseye, until the men scheduled that day of family renewal, their Catholic action floundered. Once they saw what they had stumbled on in Cana and Pre-Cana, however, once they saw the enormous interest that these movements aroused in so short a time, the direction of their energies was assured. The merger of the two groups became inevitable, for how else could marriage and the family be dealt with realistically? No one noticed that the formation of couples' groups bolted shut the possibility of going back to a program on work—the intent of Cardijn and the original idea of the six businessmen.

In retrospect one can see the impact of World War II on the decision of these men and women to apply Cardijn's Inquiry Method to the family. Like other periods of war, the early 1940s increased the strain on the family, bringing about both *more* marriages and *more unstable* marriages. Faced with the threat of separation, couples rushed into premature commitments and then were prevented by actual separation from working out necessary marital adjustments. Women became pregnant and were left to face alone the birth and rearing of children. Often they took jobs vacated by men who had gone overseas. It was no accident that the original cell of six men found in their early inquiry that divorce rates were increasing during the war (and they would peak in the year following its end).

As if in recognition of what was happening, the nation turned its thoughts after the war to family life. More people married, the men claiming the jobs they held before, the women returning to the home. The family itself was perceived as a source of fulfillment—indeed, for women, the only source of fulfillment. The good life in suburbia—four kids, swimming pool, barbecue pit, Little League, PTA (never mind father's seventy-hour work week to pay for it all)—became the dream of those riding the wave of postwar prosperity into the upper reaches of the middle class.

Many of them were Catholics. During the Second World War and until 1960, the majority of Catholics in the United States were either immigrants or children of immigrants. They were, therefore, closer than the dominant Protestant culture to life in extended (nonnuclear) family systems, whether in the old country or in the ethnic enclaves they formed in the cities of America. After the war they reaped the benefits of the GI Bill, thrived as the economy boomed, and moved into a mobile society in which the extended family was simply an encumbrance. In addition, their Church, an unquestioned authority at the time, taught that marriage was sacred (while the dominant culture was secularizing it), that it was indissoluble (but all around, divorces were on the increase), that contraception was immoral (yet it would soon become the norm). The Catholic blueprint of family behavior differed in many important respects from that of the dominant culture.

The Crowleys, of course, and many of their friends in the original action cells were not typical of this Catholic population. Their families had been in the country longer and had "made it" even before the war. They were the first of their denomination to feel the stress of mobile middle-class life and to recognize its influence on the family. They knew what it meant to pull up stakes and become a helpless nucleus in a foreign suburb. They knew the kind of isolation the Good Life can impose on young wives and mothers.

To this problem area—the family—couples' groups in Chicago, South Bend, and throughout the country brought the Christian vision that they were extensions of the collective body of Christ. Marriage, they decided, had to be kept sacred. Those institutions that affected the family—schools, churches, governments—had to be changed in order for families to flourish. The family itself had to reach outward, to be a social action unit for improving the life of the neighborhood, the city, the country. In 1956 Pat wrote in a serious vein, "We longed to implant everywhere the awareness that the family, the basic unit of society, is one of the chief means through which men are adequately directed toward their supernatural end. We wanted to keep before them the knowledge that, when Christ established the sacramental character of marriage, it was His purpose to provide a permanent pattern of society which was to stand out clearly through the many shifting forms that society might be likely to assume; to spread to the ends of the earth the love that would restore all things to Him."

In 1948 Joseph Cardijn had dinner at the suburban home of Pat and Patty Crowley. American YCW groups had decided the year before to establish national headquarters in Chicago and Monsignor Hillenbrand had been named national chairman of the movement. For Cardijn, it was a long way from the deathbed of his father and the factories of Belgium. The people with whom he shared supper and told of his work did not labor in factories; their families owned them. They were sympathetic to the worker but they were heading a movement that had turned to the family. In crossing an ocean, in leaping forty years, Cardijn's Inquiry Method—Observe-Judge-Act—had spanned much, much more.

CHAPTER SIX
THE MOMENT

Then there were four: Patsy, Mary Ann, Cathy, and Patrick, Christmas 1947.

Second anniversary of Chicago's Friendship House, 1944. Ann Harrigan, Baroness Catherine de Hueck, and Bishop Bernard Sheil are at left.

"Catholic Action" couples with Father Theodore Hesburgh, C.S.C., to the right of center.

As America changed, as its Catholic people changed, as the ideas of Joseph Cardijn took root in a few granules of new soil, subtle transformations were occurring in the lives of Pat and Patty Crowley. Old friends noticed that the two became impatient with talk of golf scores and babies, that they began to turn down social engagements because there was a meeting to attend, a conference they couldn't miss, a project they just had to finish. Regulars at the football weekends in South Bend started to wonder where Pat and Patty were. When invited to the Crowley home for dinner, those same friends were astonished by the variety of people with whom they found themselves dining.

Pat himself quit smoking, drank less, and read far more. He became a genuine student, perhaps for the first time in his life. On one occasion he wrote of that period, "We began as all young couples did, circling from one round of parties to another. But increasingly we noticed something was lacking. We liked our friends just as much, but we wanted to do something more solid and lasting with them, and with others."

Though the Crowleys were spared direct involvement in the war, they suffered minor tragedies of their own. In 1940 Patty miscarried and in 1941 she gave birth to a child who died two days later. (Puddy and Jerry Crowley lost a newborn at the same time.) Acquaintances of theirs had gone to combat and Pat's eyes were being opened at the Alien Property Custodian office. With death coming close, people began to think about the purpose of life. Those fortunate enough to remain at home felt special obligations.

In some mysterious way, Pat's conversation with Father Chick Sheedy, in which he first heard of Catholic Action, and Paul Hazard's invitation a few days later to join a businessmen's cell were answers to an inner restlessness. There *was* something he could do. Pat was instantly enthusiastic about the Inquiry Method, and when he later saw the response elicited by *Act* and the couples' groups, he was energized even further.

As a lawyer in a businessmen's cell of Catholic Action, Pat soon gained a reputation for giving free legal assistance. Newcomers to Chicago with a cause in mind and Pat's phone number in a pocket often called or appeared unannounced at his office. Pat's partners say he did too much extracurricular work; it did not actually hurt the firm, but business could have been expanded greatly.

One of the first to call on Pat was a Russian exile, the Baroness Catherine de Hueck. Having lost everything in her homeland to the communists, the Baroness had come to America, been appalled by the condition of black people, and established a Friendship House in Harlem. It was a neighborhood center where blacks and whites were welcome for food, clothes, discussions, meetings, and the planning of services to the community.

With her husband, Chicago journalist Eddie Doherty, and her friend Ann Harrigan, the Baroness came to Chicago in 1943 and set up another Friendship House in two South Side storefronts. Several years later, when their landlord told them to vacate the premises, they turned to Pat. He secured an interest-free loan from Rosary College and did the legal work that enabled them to buy and move into an old building at 4233 S. Indiana. It became Friendship House's permanent home. Later, when a black Friendship House volunteer who was in the Army was jailed for displeasing a Southern white officer, Pat, along with Leon Despres and George St. Peter, brought the case to court and proved the officer had acted illegally. The volunteer was freed.

But Pat didn't stop with legal assistance. It would be marvelous, he thought, to bring together his neighbors from the wealthy North Shore and the personnel of Friendship House. "So," Patty recalls, "the action of our group was to go to Friendship House and listen to talks. Of course, we lived in the suburbs, we didn't know any black people, and we'd go down there into this horrible section. It was bad then; it's worse now. It was scary to go down there. All black. And we'd go down to this storefront and we'd sit there. And we'd feel pretty good that we were there, but gradually we became more and more aware of how unjust our society was to black people. Of course, one of the big things you realized was that you never knew them. So one day we invited all of Friendship House up for a party in Wilmette.

"We had a lovely party, and, you know, to see black people come into our house in Wilmette that weren't maids! I guess we were talked about in Wilmette quite a bit. Rumors went all over the place: we had a fight with black people in our house supposedly. But all we had was a good time. We had a party and talked about the racial issue. We had food and drinks and singing. It was fun, it wasn't a meeting. Fortunately, Pat invited his mother and father to come. The following year they were at the home of a prominent Catholic family, and the guests started talking about what an awful thing we had done to have these black people. They didn't know that the Crowleys had been there. So they started recounting the rumors they had heard. And Mrs. Crowley—she could be like that, she could be real knifing to somebody—she said, 'It was a wonderful party. We were there.' That stopped the conversation right then."

Though the elder Crowleys did not always understand what their son and daughter-in-law were doing, they always supported it. Pat, in turn, drew continually on his parents, particularly on his father. Pat helped people and causes with legal and personal advice, but so had his father before him. Pat's CFA was the equivalent of Jerome's Knights of Columbus, his *Act* a reincarnation of the DeSoto Council *Cable*. In his thirties Pat found a stage and an audience, critical elements in the life of his father. He began to express that father, entertaining at parties as he did and going to conventions as he did. He lacked the voice and the eloquence of the elder Crowley, but he sang, made speeches, and, most important, clicked with audiences. Pat never battled his father as he changed, never left him, physically or spiritually. His father cautioned him about being taken advantage of and expressed fear that harm might come to him and his wife, but that was all.

Patty, on the other hand, was often hurt by her mother's prejudices. An incident that occurred at the beginning of Patty's involvement in the "movements" (as Mrs. Caron called them) was the first of many struggles that consumed a lifetime. "One week my mother was in town. She would come and, of course, we would want to see each other. Usually she stayed at the Drake. So she said to me, 'What are you doing tonight?' Well, we were going to Friendship House, and we just had to go down there because we had all these people from Wilmette we had encouraged to come. So we said, 'We're going to Friendship House, would you like to go with us?' We knew that she would have a fit, but what else could we do? So we had dinner with her and then we went down to Friendship House. And she went and Father Dunne gave the wildest talk you have ever heard. Oh, he gave the example of a little kid that was on a bus and some lady with a big fur coat—my mother was sitting there with a fur coat—got up and sat in a different seat because she was sitting next to a black child. Well, of course, my mother was getting madder and madder. And the Baroness gave a really lambasting talk and her language was really rough. Oh, I could just feel my mother when I was sitting there.

"Well, we drove the Baroness back, she and Eddie Doherty, and the Baroness sat there with her gum, chewing her gum all the way back. My mother never allowed us to chew gum. And she kept telling all these stories about her experiences with blacks and whites and how awful the whites were. So we dropped the Baroness off and then we dropped my mother off at the Drake. My father wasn't along and my mother started at us. She told me that I was committing a mortal sin by going down there and that in bringing other people I was responsible for their sins. Well, I was so upset! I cry very easily, especially if I get hurt like that. And I thought we were doing something right. So I cried and went home and cried and cried and cried. This was the beginning of my mother not understanding me—or us. I'm sure she blamed Pat.

"Poor Pat, he tried. He didn't know what to do with me. I remember him waking up in the middle of the night—I don't think I was asleep—and saying, 'I've got an idea, we'll take care of her.' There had been a Paulist priest in the audience who mother had talked to afterward and who she liked. So Pat said, 'We'll call the Paulist priest and we'll ask him if he would have lunch with your mother tomorrow.' My idea was I didn't want her to think I was committing sin. She didn't have to agree with me, but I didn't think it was a sin. So we called him about six in the morning because we were awake most of the night and asked if he would see my mother—if she would see him. We did it just in time because my mother hadn't slept all night either, because it had upset her. She never liked to upset me. So she called about seven in the morning and started at us, saying she was sorry and how she had done so much for us and how she loved us. So we said, 'Would you have lunch with this priest?' So she did. And that helped a lot. Because he was a nice young guy and he told her that we really weren't . . . maybe she didn't approve, but it wasn't a sin. Sin was very important in those days. Now it wouldn't make any difference.

"It was really hard for my mother—I really see it—to accept these things. You can see from her background. And I was probably . . . well, I don't think it was unjust, it was asking almost too much of her. But we began feeling very strongly about these things and we felt we could not stop just because of her."

There would be many tears in the future and Pat would always try to heal the rift. Mrs. Caron blamed him for her daughter's involvement in the movements and for her becoming (almost as bad) a Democrat, but she and her husband depended completely on his advice in other matters: what to do with the company, what to do with this child or that. Pat was the go-between for everyone in the Caron family. "And he would give them lots of time. He was very patient, and they were very demanding. You never saw Pat get mad in front of anybody. He'd come back to me and say how he felt, but he would never . . . I mean, he had plenty of reasons to get mad at my mother and things she would do. Once in a while he would get mad at me for something little, and he used to laugh at that. He'd say, 'I never get mad at anybody but you. What do I get mad at you for?'

"I'm sure that's the same as his father. His father had a very good disposition. Pat, you see, always had a very good attitude toward life. You know, to live by the day. That was his mother's statement. I was the worrier. That's my nature, to worry about things. And, of course, I learned from him how to get by. And he'd get annoyed when I'd get worried. He'd say, 'You can't worry.' If you had contact with him, you just didn't let things bother you."

Those who saw Pat and Patty live and work together say she was the energizer, the organizer, the "motor." "More efficient," they say, "more intense," "far shrewder," "more profound," "more abrasive" even. Pat had the wide-eyed curiosity of a college freshman sitting at a bar, willing to try anything, if only for a lark. "Oh boy, let's have a convention," he would say with glee, and Patty would coordinate the incredible detail that made the convention happen. The daughter of a strict but affectionate father who was away far too often, she never wanted to be apart from Pat. In their marriage the ambition and worry of the O. J. Carons complemented the ease and warmth of the Jerome Crowleys. Hers was the animus, his the anima.

Yet little might have come of the energies that emerged from their union were it not for the last week of March, 1947. On March 24, a week after she had organized registration at the important meeting of family-life directors, Patty gave birth to their fourth child and third daughter, Catherine Ann (CA for Catholic Action, Pat had to quip). Mother and child were fine at first, but then Patty started to hemorrhage. One night she became very ill, received the last sacraments, and was sent to surgery. For many hours it was touch and go, but in the morning it seemed as though she would live. Gradually, over the ensuing months, she regained her health.

It was the turning point of the Crowleys' life and the moment that sealed their commitment. Some of those Pat called to ask for prayers say they had never heard him so dejected or worried. But others remember a remarkable serenity, an implicit faith in Patty's eventual recovery.

The impact on Patty was awesome. "It was a traumatic thing for Pat. Everything was happening so fast. Everyone was around my bed doing something, but all I had to do was think. I thought I was going to die. When you are there, and conscious, and you think you're almost gone, you really do think about the life you have led and, you know, I hadn't done very much. You think that, well, you haven't got much time, there are so many things to be done. If I lived, I had better start. I think after that it was our gratitude that I didn't die. I always say people should almost die once."

Patty had done so twice, once as a child (and it made a deep impression on her mother) and once as a mother herself. Not only was she affected this time by a sudden review of her life, she—and Pat—were profoundly moved by the support of friends in their Catholic Action cells. "Pat called a couple of people and asked them to pray. Evidently everybody prayed. There was one couple—Pat and I have never forgotten it—who stayed up all night long. The Stones. A simple working-class family. They really stayed up all night on their knees. You don't believe things like that. Even though I haven't seen them in years and years, I still feel close to them." That sense of connection, that feeling of being with others who are for you, no matter where in the city or where on the planet they lived, was to characterize the rest of the Crowleys' life.

Pat and Patty came back from death grateful for life and aware of its short duration. The ideas to which they had been exposed in the previous four years were no longer a source of excitement; they were a basis for commitment, the seriousness of which Pat's light touch might lead one to overlook. One of the beliefs became paramount. "Somebody gave us the idea that, when something comes to you, you should accept it because it has come for a reason. And then you do the best you can. And sometimes you make a fool of yourself. You really do. Because you know you aren't the one; you know other people who are much more capable than you are.

"People would come and we'd say, 'Come up for dinner.' We'd always get people over to talk. Oh, we had marvelous discussions on what they were doing. I remember Father Klakovitch from Yugoslavia coming up one time, spreading his maps about communism all over the living room, and saying how it was going to take over the whole world. He was a very right-wing guy. So there were a lot of different kinds of people that came into our lives. I don't know, I'm sure we should have said no lots of times. That was the thing that Mr. Crowley was always afraid of, that we were going to have somebody come that would do us harm or take advantage of us.

"But why would you be asked? I mean you look back and it was just the hand of the Lord. All of these people coming and visiting, why did they come?"

It wasn't always easy. "The kids would often be screaming." And those same children would say without hesitation in the years ahead that their parents *were* taken advantage of. But Patty tells the story of one of many foreign students who came to Chicago and appeared at Pat's law office. "The guy didn't have a cent of money and it turned out he had a disease. Pat called me and said, 'Maybe this is one I shouldn't bring home.' I said, 'Bring him home. We'll do something with him.' We kept him for a while—he was very sick—and gave him one of Patrick's suits. The guy went on to get his doctorate and has been a great person. And we didn't get the disease!

"Probably we shouldn't have done it all the time. But we always felt we never sought it out and . . ."

And . . . there is a reason. Why else would you be asked? When Pat would write or speak of their activities in the years to come, he would always do so in a constructive tone. "You can spend your life fighting those who want to tear down," he would say, "or you can spend your life building up. I believe it is better to build." When asked why his children were good children, he would reply, "Well, I tell them every day what good kids they are and they just want to prove I'm right." But his sense of assurance, his ease, his constant willingness to encourage should not deflect one's gaze from an inner toughness, a persistence, a courage, a capacity for hard work, a willingness to try one thing after another. These are the qualities one sees in his enormous correspondence, in the diaries he kept as he and his wife (and, often enough, his family) crisscrossed the country (and later circled the globe), recruiting supporters, fighting skirmishes, linking one person to another. Pat and Patty had been to the brink one moment in 1947, and they were fortunate and grateful that they did not go over.

Childerley Retreat House in Wheeling, Illinois—birthplace of CFM.

Pat and Patty with the "Yellow Book." The price had already been raised to fifty cents.

CHAPTER SEVEN
CFM IS BORN

A dinner for CFM couples and chaplains. Third from the right is Father John Egan, appointed chaplain of Chicago's Cana and Pre-Cana in 1946.

Hula hoops invade the 1956 Notre Dame convention.

Father Louis Putz, C.S.C., and Father William McManus of Chicago as CFM becomes international.

Malta, 1956.

Uruguay, 1957.

As the inner lives of the Crowleys came together and took direction, so did the lives of disparate Catholic Action cells concerned with family life, throughout the country. One of the magnets drawing them together was a booklet produced by the Chicago group on the advice of Monsignor Hillenbrand—and his "advice" could be very authoritative. "Whether it's good or not," he said of the booklet, "get it out."

They got it out. Clem Lane, a journalist for the *Chicago Daily News* coordinated the writing; Fathers Gerard Weber and James Kilgallen spoke for the clergy; Hillenbrand himself took care of the *Imprimatur* (the ecclesiastical guarantee, so important in those days, that the book was free of moral or doctrinal error); the Crowleys and a few others put up the money; and in 1949 *For Happier Families: How to Start a C. F. A. Section* was ready. "Hundreds of Catholic families have found a way to greater happiness," it began. They have done so by forming sections of Christian Family Action to do battle with the forces of secularism. "When the newspaper becomes the family bible, when the radio becomes the family altar, when the movie screen replaces the pulpit as the teacher of morals and manners, that's Secularism."

The challenge was to make the family and its setting more Christian, to do so as members of the lay apostolate in concert with pope and bishops and priests. *For Happier Families* laid out the method, step by step. First, get a chaplain. Second, choose like-minded couples from the parish. "They do not have to be holy Joes, just the regular people." Third, begin meeting every other week, rotating the chairmanship until the group settles on a leader. Fourth, schedule meetings of the leaders from various groups on alternate weeks.

The group meetings were to follow a precise format: opening prayer, Gospel inquiry (15 minutes), liturgy (15 minutes), social inquiry (45 minutes), preparation for the next meeting, chaplain's remarks, closing prayer. During the Gospel inquiry members were to discuss a passage from Scripture, asking themselves questions suggested by the booklet. During the liturgy they were to do the same with a passage from the encyclical on the Mystical Body or the mass. The social inquiry was the point of insertion of Cardijn's method. One *observed*—his neighborhood, for example: "How many of your neighbors can you call by name, or do you know something about?" One *judged* in the light of the Gospel: "What do you think knowing our neighbors and their needs, and trying to fill these needs, has to do with Christ's words: 'As long as you did it to one of these My least brethren, you did it to Me?' " One *acted:* "Make a list of your neighbors and what you know about them; give a summary report at the next meeting." The next meeting would continue from there, the long-range goal being a program of service, everything from organized political activity to simple shows of kindness, to make the neighborhood a more nurturant setting for the family.

The manual was simple, untheoretical, practical, prescriptive (down to advice about refreshments), buoyant with promises of "new zest, new purpose to life." People would read a news release in their diocesan paper, send thirty-five cents to Room 1808, 100 West Monroe, Chicago, and receive a copy. In August, 1949, *Act* proudly reported that 2,300 copies of the "Yellow Book" had been distributed in one hundred cities, among them Paris. The Crowleys had acquired a list of interested Catholic laity, proving the wisdom of Hillenbrand's directive.

An equally wise move was the calling of a conference of Catholic Action representatives in June, 1949. Planned at the Crowley house the winter before, it drew over sixty people to the Childerley Retreat House in Wheeling, Illinois. There were delegates from men's groups, women's groups, and couples' groups, along with several chaplains. Among the latter were Father Theodore Hesburgh, who had just completed a dissertation on Catholic Action and was working with a group of World War II veterans at Notre Dame, and Father Louis Putz, chaplain of the South Bend group started by Burnie and Helene Bauer. Eleven delegations in all, they came from cities like Milwaukee, Cleveland, St. Paul, New York, Nashville, Fond du Lac, Wisconsin, and (shades of O. J. Caron!) Woonsocket, Rhode Island.

It was a stormy gathering. Representatives argued about the name they would adopt (was it to be Christian Family Action or Christian Family Movement?), about membership (was it to be couples only?) and about the use of the Cardijn technique (was it, and was social action, an essential component?). A rift developed between the "rich" and the "poor." Woonsocket's Armand Beausoleil, for example, was a mill worker interested in cooperative family ventures that saved money on food, clothing, and shelter. But these concerns were never discussed by a conference dominated by business and professional couples.

Despite the friction, delegates did agree to establish a national coordinating committee, to make *Act* the official publication of the organization—whatever its name, membership, and method of operating—and by a last-minute vote of six to five, to make the Crowleys temporary chairpersons. They also decided it wouldn't hurt to meet the following year. And so, in a most inauspicious way, an international movement was born.

St. Procopius College in Lisle, Illinois, was the scene of a second meeting in 1950. Even though more delegates came as couples, the sleeping arrangements were hardly conducive to "happier families." The men stayed at the college and kept each other awake with their snoring while the women, most of them pregnant, bedded down in dormitory fashion in a large hall across the street, keeping each other awake by getting up throughout the night. Married or not, man and woman did not sleep together on a Catholic campus in 1950.

The bleary eyed conventioneers, however, were able to make some decisions. The name of their organization would be Christian Family Movement (CFM); here the Crowleys and their fellow Chicagoans made a concession. Membership would be restricted to couples and the Cardijn method would be mandatory; when some groups threatened to drop out as a result, Pat said, let them go. Nor did he or the convention budge when a monsignor from St. Paul, who had forbidden his leader couple to attend, insisted that priests rather than laity represent an area. Pat may have been easygoing and able to compromise, but it was clear to those gathered that he also knew how to be firm. Once again he and Patty were chosen to head the movement as executive secretary couple, a position they were to hold for twenty years.

Because of Crowley connections with Notre Dame and its president, Father John Cavanaugh, the convention moved to the South Bend campus in 1951. Not only were the accommodations inexpensive, but couples were allowed to sleep in the same room! One hundred of them attended that year and heard a report that ninety-seven cities, including Tokyo, Copenhagen, London, and several in Latin America, had action groups. CFM was now on solid footing. It was headed by a couple many would later describe as charismatic. It had a hospitable setting for its annual convention. Soon children would join their parents for the summer get-togethers, and the numbers in attendance would swell.

The summer conventions came to be CFM's occasion for introducing an Inquiry program for the coming year. It had been decided at St. Procopius (the Crowleys lost some close friends over the matter) to augment *For Happier Families* with an annual booklet whose theme changed each year. New groups would continue to use the "Yellow Book" and direct the Inquiry Method toward their own neighborhoods. Groups beyond their first year would use the new manuals. In 1950-51 the program topic was "Economics of the Family," a choice that drove the monsignor from St. Paul away for good. An Inquiry book was written that outlined meeting by meeting, question by question, a series of Observes, Judges, and Actions related to the cost of living, credit-buying, housing, employment, and so on.

The choice of themes for the annual booklet became the subject of heated discussion. Each year, after *Act* had solicited the opinion of CFMers, a program committee met in January to make the decision. Half a dozen couples, several chaplains, and Monsignor Hillenbrand, now the national chaplain, would gather at the Crowleys or at Childerley, select a topic, and then argue over every word that went into the manual. These were trying meetings. Even though Hillenbrand was the movement's spiritual guide and the one who could provide the *Imprimatur,* he could be very difficult to work with—ill at ease with women, harsh, autocratic, set in his opinions. Some of the other chaplains were just as stubborn. Once, when all of them failed to appear at a session, one of the lay representatives cracked, "Good. Now we can get some work done."

Some of the annual programs were entitled "Social Responsibility and Education," "The Layman's Role in the Church," "Social Harmony: Respecting Minorities," and "International Life." The "poor" delegates had little use for many of these themes. People overwhelmed by daily living, they insisted, did not have time to fight for the United Nations or do missionary work on the other side of the tracks. Getting the streets paved and starting clothing exchanges were far more important. But, since the well-to-do were footing the bills for the meetings or holding them at their homes, the others felt powerless to press their views and began to drop out.

Most CFMers, however, welcomed the annual inquiry programs. Along with *Act,* which increased to six issues a year in 1952, and the Notre Dame conventions, the introductory and yearly manuals brought coherence to an otherwise disparate array of middle-class Catholics impressed with the possibilities of their role as laity and troubled in some vague way about family life.

Another source of unity to the movement was the Crowleys themselves, who tried to visit everyone who had written for a copy of *For Happier Families.* Pat's work for the Caron and O'Brien companies demanded a good deal of travel, so he and Patty and sometimes the children would climb into the station wagon for jaunts all over the country. It was business during the day, CFM work in the evening and on weekends. They wrote people on their list ahead of time, saying they just happened to be coming through and would like to talk to some couples about the book. "Oh, we had a lot of nerve," Patty recalls. "We'd use any excuse to try to meet with couples. And a lot of the meetings were not successes, believe me. We didn't make a big hit in some of the places." No matter what the outcome, Pat kept a detailed diary of names, places, reactions, ways of following up each contact.

In those days one checked with the pastor of a parish and even the bishop of a diocese before meeting with the laity under their jurisdiction. Sometimes a bishop denied them permission to organize. Sometimes a pastor objected to the idea of men and women meeting together and, on top of that, discussing Scripture. How were they, after all, to know the correct interpretation of a passage? The Crowleys could have ignored the hierarchy and the clergy, but Pat was too much of a diplomat and too wise a politician for that. Besides, he had a way of gently deflating a puffed-up prelate, of talking down to him even without his knowing it, of camouflaging a serious message with an innocent witticism. The Crowleys never failed to recruit among the clergy. Though they had run-ins with the Bishops' Family Life Bureau, they attended its meetings and in 1957 were appointed to its advisory board. They made their pitch to any priest who would listen. It was a first when Pat, Patty, and Peter and Alma Fitzpatrick addressed a gathering of California seminarians in 1951, but visits to seminaries were soon a regular occurrence, complete with singing by the Crowley children. Seminarians were potential chaplains.

Their trips had their light moments—the kids hoping the next place would not serve ham like the previous six, Mary Ann crying her lungs out in the bedroom of a tiny house while Pat talked to a group of strangers, his hosts, about happy families. When their travels eventually brought them to Woonsocket, Rhode Island, Pat told a large gathering that Patty's grandfather had lived there, and for want of something better to say, added that he "hadn't stolen the place." After the meeting someone came up to him and said in all seriousness that, yes, O. J.'s father didn't take that money from the Knights of Columbus. For once in his life, Pat was struck dumb.

Patty remembers audiences howling throughout his talks. "I heard Pat give many, many talks and every time he gave the same line. Everybody thought everything he said was a riot because he did have a way of saying a very simple thing in a funny way. He'd go on and on and on and tell the same story I don't know how many times. But I always laughed. I guess that was part of our act. And Pat would say, 'Well, she's heard this a million times, but she still thinks it's good, so it must be pretty good.'"

"Ma" would nudge him because he was carrying on too long, and then she would add some serious thoughts of her own. She liked to talk to audiences rather than read from a prepared text. "Pat always called me 'Ma.' Always. Even when we were younger. After a talk he wondered whether he said very much, but then they always remembered the things he said. Years later I heard people say they didn't remember all the serious stuff he might have said, but they always remembered his stories." Pat's offhand manner had another effect: it made him extraordinarily difficult to oppose.

On their return home, the Crowleys would be greeted by stacks of accumulated mail. "We'd like to start a group in Grand Rapids. What do we do?" "Our group of three couples is breaking down. Could you stop by?" "I'm going back to Japan and want to begin something there." "What are the names of some contact couples in Los

Angeles?" "Our group is going so well now." Initiatives, successes, failures: people poured themselves out in their letters, and everyone was answered. Anyone in CFM who wished could have direct contact with the leader couple. For years Patty and her close friend Dorothy Drish did the secretarial work; then Helen Fagan, Lois Heidbrink, and Helen Bauer were hired as full-time secretaries. Never did the Crowleys refuse an opportunity to make a personal connection with a CFM couple.

The two, of course, had the freedom and the money to support their CFM activities. Pat's duties for Caron and O'Brien were discharged as easily on the road as in the office. Emily, Effie, and Sarah, who did the housecleaning and laundry, were available to stay with the children, and all were trusted. When Pat and Patty traveled, they stayed at the homes of other couples. When they had large meetings at their own home, they put their children up with neighbors. For several years the Crowleys absorbed much of CFM's printing, postage, and secretarial costs. In 1952, despite stout objections, *Act* asked for a dollar a year per couple; but even as CFM attempted to stand on its own, Pat and Patty were always there to raise money and contribute some of their own.

In 1955 the editorship of *Act* passed to Don and Barbara Thorman. They were to serve in that capacity for nine years, and he would go on to edit the *National Catholic Reporter*. In the midfifties *Act* was still a newsletter that bore the personality of Pat Crowley. It encouraged, advised, passed on anecdotes and corny jokes. It reported news of successful meetings and overlooked failures or behind-the-scenes conflict. It opposed contraception, encouraged large families, and wrote neutrally of working mothers. There were maps showing the spread of CFM, question-and-answer boxes that provided tips on how to handle people who talked too much, homilies by chaplains, and (absolutely essential) reports of what CFMers were *doing*. In Santa Cruz an action group helped a family move. In nearby Watsonville a credit union was formed. In South Portland, Maine, two groups "adopted" a mother and her small children. In Delphos, Ohio, the St. John's group set up home entertainment to keep teenagers away from the night-spots. In Portland, Oregon, CFMers volunteered their services to Friendship House. In Aylmer, Quebec, a cell invited old and handicapped persons to a parish social. On Chicago's North Side, a group from St. Margaret Mary's ordered subscriptions to local papers for all the community's servicemen. In Peekskill, New York, ten CFMers worked on a state housing survey to bring about low-cost housing for low-income families. There was no controversy, but plenty of cheers. *Act* and Pat Crowley were protective and proud of CFM.

In 1956, the movement passed a number of statistical milestones. Over a thousand, including chaplains and children, attended that year's convention. *Act* had become a monthly and had a readership of close to twenty thousand couples. The annual budget surpassed thirty thousand dollars, the number of chaplains, seven hundred. The movement's organizational chart, too, had increased in complexity. The executive secretary couple—Pat and Patty—chaired the Executive Committee of the National Coordinating Committee, composed of presidents of various federations. Federations, roughly equivalent to dioceses, were made up of delegates from sections. Sections consisted of leaders of action groups, the basic cell in CFM. Some of these leaders were also known as "contact couples" because they received announcements from national headquarters. The coordinating committee had delegated some of its work to a program committee, charged with preparing the annual inquiry books, and to a board of publications, which handled the finances of *Act, For Happier Families,* the inquiry books, and a plethora of brochures and pamphlets. One could purchase manuals for chaplains, manuals for action group leaders, automobile stickers, cuff links, pendants, and lapel pins. There were conventions and newsletters at the federation, as well as the national, level. All in all, it was a heady brew of euphoria.

The highlight of 1956, however, was a six-week tour of the world during which Pat and Patty spread the message of CFM. In years previous the two had been host to many foreign visitors, some of whom returned to their countries to start units of CFM. In January, 1956, the Crowleys set out to do by plane what they had done by station wagon just a few years before—visit as many CFM couples and recruit as many newcomers as possible.

Pat wrote a newsletter along the way, setting down some of the lightness and some of the seriousness of his soul, some of its openness and some of its inevitable provinciality.

January 28, Los Angeles: "This report will be sent to a few people who asked to hear of the tour and to a few more who we thought might enjoy sharing the experience with us. No one will be quizzed on these documents."

January 30, Honolulu: "One guest turned out to be the father of Grace Kelly, so we couldn't resist telling the group that we had a commission from Father Egan to sign Grace and her Prince up for a Pre-Cana."

February 2, Tokyo: "They said it's hard to get the women to the meetings and that the women don't take too much part in discussions. We did tell them they take longer than the Irish to say good-night."

February 7, Hong Kong: "What contrasts are made by the terrible poverty and the magnificent homes of the Chinese, English, and Americans."

February 8, Manila: "Three groups were organized on the spot. Even Billy Graham (who, incidentally, has been trailing us) couldn't ask for a better response."

February 12, Saigon: "We visited a hut filled with blind people and saw tragic sights that will ever remind us how good God is to us and how grateful we should be. These people need our prayers and help. Let's hope their flight from communism will be better rewarded than seems evident from our visit."

February 13, Singapore: "We have flown over water for literally days. What a way to realize how small and insignificant we really are and, conversely, how great is He who created all of this!"

February 17, Bombay: "They are talking about making Hindi the language of the country, but very few people know it. How sad that prejudice against the Western world would even suggest such a crazy course of conduct."

February 21, Beirut: "We were overwhelmed by all the Moslem devotion. These people pray five times each day, usually in public. They carry prayer beads in their hands and have no shame about showing their devotion. They have one weakness: women are second-rate citizens."

February 23, Jerusalem: "This was the crowning experience to pray where Our Lord redeemed us and where the Mass was instituted."

February 24, Cairo: "We are overwhelmed at the thought of U.S. responsibility in the maze of international intrigue. It would appear that Britain knows the tricks while we put up the dough."

March 1, Rome: "His Holiness was most simple and gracious. He gave us about three minutes during which time we handed him the white, leatherbound copies of all the literature and all copies of *Act.*"

March 5, Brussels: "The JOC group was made up of a mailman, a railroad man, a chemist, a factory worker, several government functionaries and clerks. We expressed regrets that there were no lawyers and assured them that lawyers weren't so high class and could learn much from them."

March 8, Paris: "We picked up many good ideas from the Equipes and hope to get some more. They acknowledged that they have lifted some from us."

March 16, Dublin: "The last day in Europe. We wonder whether some of the things reported might not sound a bit too positive. We'll close with one more word of thanks to our dear Lord for making this possible. We hope this trip has been good for CFM. We know it had been a rare privilege for the P. F. C.'s."

Unabashed religious sentiment, irrepressible boyish enthusiasm, reports telling of speeches to Catholic college students, seminarians, businessmen, connection after connection with Catholic couples, workers, clerics, cardinals. Most of the contacts were with the well-to-do in these countries, not because the Crowleys avoided the poor (on the contrary, they thought CFM would benefit rich and poor alike), but because what they were saying "took" with professionals rather than paupers, just as it had at home. The Crowleys were quick to follow up their 1956 tour. In June, 1957, they brought their four children to the first convention of the *Movimento Familiar Cristiano* (MFC) in Montevideo, Uruguay. Delegates from Uruguay, Argentina, Chile, Brazil, Paraguay, Cuba, Spain and Venezuela were already using *Por una Familia más Feliz,* the Spanish edition of *For Happier Families.* In October of the same year Pat and Patty attended the Second World Congress of the Laity in Rome and were awarded the *Pro Ecclesia et Pontifice* medal by Pius XII. In 1958 they went to Paris to represent CFM at the World Family Congress sponsored by the International Union of Family Organizations. By the end of that year, CFM was active in twenty-six foreign countries.

At home the movement continued to grow, each year's convention the "biggest ever." Controversy, heretofore kept under the table, began to be aired in public. Hillenbrand was dissatisfied that the movement was lodged in the middle class and would not take root among workers and nonwhites. He wanted the annual programs to move beyond family and neighborhood to concentrate on race, social justice, and international problems. At conventions Putz would ask what happened to the social action thrust of CFM. Was the movement simply a club, a place where mobile Catholics could meet and be with their own kind, a mechanism by which families could make social adjustments and be "happier?" Others charged that CFM recruited everybody in sight; membership was by a revolving door; hence, it could not escape the dilemma of "all talk and no action." Still others thought the inquiry books shallow. They did not face the complexity of social problems and did not allow for sustained commitment to a problem.

When *Act* began in 1959 to allow gentle "constructive criticism," readers told of "slavish following of the manual," complained that all they did in their meetings was "flutter past" problems and bemoaned a decline in enthusiasm after the first year. Some said there was not enough spiritual training, some that their group engaged in no concerted action. Too much politics, said some: of the twenty-five inquiries in the introductory book, only nine deal with the family. Too communistic, said others: the 1960-61 program on international life exalts the United Nations, which is infested with communists. And if the readers disagreed with CFM's politics, they also took objection to its endorsement of nursery school during Sunday mass for noisy three-year-olds.

Patty admits that she and Pat "were always very defensive of CFM. And it was always criticized. Sometimes we were criticized because we were considered bourgeois. What did we know about things? There was a snobbery that the workers were better than CFM because we had more money. We always fought that. Then the movement was criticized because we'd do something and we weren't doing it right. We resented anybody that pulled people out of CFM. Naturally, if you believe in something, you don't like it to be criticized.

"I'm sure that CFM should have been criticized. I think one of the problems was that we had this great method of Observe-Judge-Act, but we never practiced it perfectly. We were always struggling with how you bring in 'observes.' If you were meeting on recreation for children, for instance, during the week you were supposed to find out and bring back to the next meeting the facts of what recreational facilities existed for children in the neighborhood. Not just guess at it, but go out and talk to the schools or the Park Board and bring back the exact facts. But people are human, and two weeks go by and you haven't done your 'observes.' And then you judge. Is this the way things should be if it were a good neighborhood, or if you were doing it the way . . . we usually brought Christ in. Then there was always the action. And a lot of people didn't do the action. We were criticized sometimes that we talked and didn't do anything."

CFM was a loose, decentralized organization (which is how the Crowleys wanted it) and therefore difficult to motivate and difficult to steer. One could marvel at the diversity of political ideologies housed within its ill-defined walls. Unlike many others who held national office in the movement, Pat and Patty always remained in their local action group. Their numerous individual contacts kept them in touch with the grass roots and laid the foundation for enormous personal influence. In the final analysis, however, local groups were free to go their own way.

Go their own way they did, but never far enough to remove coherence from the movement, at least as the 1950s closed. Controversy at that point did not debilitate CFM but contributed to its vitality. Conventions continued to draw even more impressive speakers ("You gotta have the fan dancers," said Pat when planning the annual event.) In 1959, twenty-four hundred endured an intense August heat wave to hear Senator Eugene McCarthy introduce an inquiry on "Politics and Christian Life" by exhorting parents to "lead young people away from the popular disposition to be cynical about politics and politicians." Ten years before, sixty delegates had struggled to the initial meeting at Childerley.

Early in 1961, Pat and Monsignor Hillenbrand had lunch with Bolton Sullivan, president of Skil Corporation and a parishioner of Hillenbrand's, and persuaded him to donate an abandoned factory on the West Side of Chicago to CFM, YCW, and YCS. Money was raised to renovate the building, and the three organizations had a national headquarters at 1655 West Jackson. It was sorely needed, even though it meant that Patty had to commute to the city every day instead of working in her home.

All the élan CFM felt in this, the first decade of its life, was part of a larger renaissance. In the 1950s American Catholics, half of them still immigrants or the children of immigrants, were coming abreast of their countrymen socially and economically—a fact symbolized by John Kennedy's election in 1960. Catholic schools, churches, and seminaries were overflowing, religious goods stores and publishing houses flourishing. The first *For Happier Families* had warned about secularism; but the nation, as it moved to the suburbs, was actually experiencing a religious revival and a renewal of interest in the family. For those who wanted society to change, the prospects *never* seemed better: freedom rides and sit-ins in the South, our youngest president creating a Peace Corps and pledging to have a man on the moon by the end of the decade.

And in Rome, on January 25, 1959, a newly elected pope who was supposed to serve a nondescript interim made the dramatic announcement of an ecumenical council. He wanted, he said, to let some fresh air into the Church. It would prove to be quite a gust, for it had been building for decades in places like a factory in Belgium, a home in Wilmette, a retreat house in Illinois, a campus in Indiana, a parish hall in Japan, a mansion in Uruguay.

Pat turns forty-one. Two foster children and Patsy stand in rear. "Algie" Augustine, Patrick, Cathy, and Mary Ann watch from up close.

CHAPTER EIGHT
THE TWO WORLDS OF AL AUGUSTINE

1955—the first Christmas with Theresa. Dinh Tran, a student from Vietnam, was living with the Crowleys at the time.

Al and his mother at Notre Dame.

"I was born in Lithuania and my father died in Germany. Lithuania was a border country during the war and the Russians came in and wiped out the Germans, and the Germans came back on their march toward Russia and pushed the Russians out. When the Russians were coming back once again, a lot of Lithuanians, including my mother and father, decided they wanted out. My father was the warden of the largest prison in Lithuania so he had to get out for political reasons. He left, and my mother left a while afterward and met him in Germany. He died in Germany. She used to say he was murdered because he had a lot of money. He fell off a train—fell off, pushed off, whatever. Then we came to the United States. My mother had to work, and there was nowhere for little Al to go. One thing happened after another and I ended up at the Crowleys through the foster parent program of Catholic Charities.

"The earliest recollection of my life takes place in the backyard of the Crowleys. I remember being on a swing in the backyard. It was the day my mother brought me to the Crowleys for the first time. I remember how she was going to leave, and I knew she was going to leave, and I was really upset. All of a sudden she was gone. I remember they were all getting ready for dinner and I wasn't going to eat. It was horrible. Patsy came out and talked me into coming inside. I thought she was nice. I don't remember all the words she said, but I remember she was so nice, and she talked me into going inside.

"I was supposed to stay there a year, but my mother liked the Crowleys so much and thought they were such a good influence on me that she begged them to allow me to stay. It was such a nice place for me to grow up, in the suburbs. She was living in the bad parts of Chicago. So that went on, on a yearly basis. Every summer I'd go back to live with my mother and that was going to be it. About August I would start getting lonely, because I was used to having people around and it was just my mother and myself. And then she'd say, 'Do you want to go back?' And I'd say, 'Well, I like being with you, but I'd like to go back.' And then I'd go back to the different life again.

"So I stayed with the Crowleys until my mother got remarried, when I was getting ready to start sixth grade. Then I went back to live with my mother and her new husband. I went to school on the South Side of Chicago, grammar school, and then I started high school. During those years, really, I had very limited contact with the Crowleys. But I kept in touch with them on a periodic basis.

"My mother had married a guy who was an alcoholic and a real bum. I'd been opposed to it. I remember talking to her from the Crowleys' house when she said she was going to get married. She told me on the phone. I told her what a horrible mistake it was. All the wisdom of a fifth grader saying, 'Mother, the guy's a bum.' But she loved him and wanted to do it.

"About the middle of my junior year of high school it got so bad with fights around the house, I couldn't handle it: me threatening to kill myself, my mother getting beaten up by him. I tried to kill him one time when he was beating her up. I dragged him off her and started strangling him and said to myself, 'What are you doing, you're crazy.' So I ran away from home—my home on the South Side—and didn't know where to go. I called the Crowleys. 'I don't know where to go. Can I come up and stay with you for a little while, until I figure out what I'm doing?' And they said sure. So I ended up staying there the next year and a half, the rest of my high school. I commuted from Wilmette to St. Rita's on the South Side, about an hour and a half each way every day. I wanted to finish up where I started.

"Then Mr. Crowley got me into Notre Dame. Arranged a scholarship for me, not a big one, but a couple thousand dollars, big enough that it allowed me to go there. So I went to Notre Dame and got involved in a lot of the sort of things they were involved in. I became president of YCS and things like that. Went to all the conventions. We had a great group there: six people who in our senior year ran the whole university. All the big officers in the school came from our little YCS group, because it's such good training.

"I graduated from Notre Dame and went to Illinois law school. Got out of law school and went to practice with Dad's (Pat's) law firm. I was there for five years until I decided there was an opportunity to go and do something, the kind of thing I think I might like to do—regulate professionals and get rid of the bums."

Algimantis Kasimiris Augustinavicius was two months old when his mother fled Lithuania and the oncoming Russians. The wife of a wealthy prison warden, she had been (or at least had been trained to be) both an athlete and an opera singer. Ironically, because she had been born in Russia, she used a Russian immigration visa to escape the Russians and come to the United States. When she arrived, her infant son was six months old. She had lost homeland, husband, and fortune.

In order to work she placed her son in an orphanage and began to look for a foster home through Catholic Social Services. It was 1948, the year Joseph Cardijn came to the Crowley home for dinner, the year before the first CFM meeting at Childerley. The Crowleys had four children at the time. Cathy was a year old, Patrick three, Mary Ann four, and Patsy eight. Patty had fully recovered from her near-fatal hemorrhage of the year before. "After Cathy," she says, "we couldn't have any more children and we were really upset (which is sort of a laugh today when nobody wants more than two). We decided that we wanted to have more, and somebody told us about foster children. So we called the Catholic Charities to see if we could get a foster child. Al was our first."

The idea did not sit well with Grandmother Marietta Caron. The Crowleys, in fact, kept news of Al from the Carons until a fellow poker-clubber at a Notre Dame football game let it slip. "How's Al?" he said, greeting Pat and Patty. He turned to congratulate the elder Carons on their new grandson.

"Al?" interrupted Mrs. Caron, her eyebrows lifting. "Who's Al?"

Pat shot his friend a glance, and he got the message. "Al, uh, you know, Mrs. Caron, how's the Al-gae in your swimming pool?"

Mrs. Caron wasn't fooled for a minute and was on the phone the next day, very agitated. Four children are enough, she said, your father was one of twelve and most of them starved, you'll only get in trouble. It was nearly as bad as the time the Baronness de Hueck chewed gum and excoriated white people in fur coats. But Patty survived the onslaught once again, and out of the incident came a new name for their foster child—Algie, you know, like the stuff in your swimming pool.

The children who were old enough remember his coming vividly, for after it everything changed. Algie was the first of a string of visitors who became their friends (and their rivals), who played with them (and took their toys), who slept next to them (and forced them on the floor), who were going to stay a few months (but remained for years). The year that Algie came was also the year that Pat and Patty stepped up their CFA, Cana, and Pre-Cana activities. The pace at 2304 Elmwood, Wilmette, was quickening. The quarters were getting crowded.

Most of the children knew only the life of meetings, singing, three in a bedroom, and little elbow room at dinner. Patsy, who was in fourth grade when Algie arrived, had some appreciation of the change. She was sent to boarding school with the Sacred Heart nuns when her mother was sick, returned after she improved, and soon thereafter welcomed the Crowleys' first permanent visitor. "His mother came, brought him in, and we all sat at the table. We knew that she was going to leave him. So my friend and I were in charge of distracting Algie. We had him out on the swings in back. She didn't say good-bye to him. She just left him. He knew, I think. He was only three. All of a sudden his mother wasn't there, and then he cried."

Each year brought more children. Virginia and Margaret, two Italian girls, joined Algie in his second year. When they left, the confusion increased: Mary Ann and Cathy were confronted with a pair of sisters named Mary Ann and Kathy. Usually there were seven children at home, counting the Crowleys' four. Though Algie was the only one they asked for, once he arrived Catholic Charities kept calling to see if there was room for more. Occasionally friends would call, knowing of a couple having trouble with their marriage and . . . "could you take their children until they get straightened out?" It was hard to say no. After all, if someone asked, there had to be a reason.

The smaller the children who came into the Crowleys' home, the better their own children liked it. Infants and toddlers, however, were hard to come by. An exception was Michael Smith, all two and-a-half years of him, the only boy other than Algie the Crowleys ever took. He was a delight for the few months he was in their home and even sang during the family presentations to push CFM. Once he soloed for a group of Maryknoll seminarians who couldn't help but smile and chuckle throughout his performance. Michael became indignant and shouted at them, "It's not funny." And that, to Michael's dismay, brought the house down.

Pat and Patty took ten foster children in all, each for about a year. "It was probably crazy," Patty says in retrospect. "I must say we were always sort of glad when they left. It was a relief, but then we went and took another one."

Their own children loved to see new playmates arrive, but after a few weeks the guests often seemed like invaders. Patsy was fortunate enough to be older than the newcomers, so she could act as a mother and not feel intruded upon—at least most of the time. Cathy, the youngest, got along with everybody. But the experience was difficult for Mary Ann and Patrick. Mary Ann became, in her own words, "a loner" lost in the shuffle. Patrick, who had reading problems in school, suffered in comparison with Algie, who was brighter. "Patrick had a hard time with that," says Mary Ann. "He used to come and tell me about that." After Algie, all the foster children were from broken homes, and they were emotionally wearing. With them came periodic visits from social workers to make sure the Crowleys weren't mistreating their wards. (Patty never understood why they worked on *her* instead of on the childrens' parents.) When parents wanted to visit their children, they had to be entertained—sometimes fended off. There was constant worry that the older children, the hardest to handle, would run away. On occasion they did, and Pat and Patty took off in pursuit.

In such an atmosphere the Crowley children came to value time alone with their mother and father, especially with Dad. Patsy, the oldest, captured more than the others. "I used to love to talk to my father at night. My mother always went to bed early, but my father used to stay up, and I can remember talking to him in the kitchen about different kids. He would see my point of view on some things—or Mary Ann's, because I could understand what Mary Ann was going through, because that was hard. The thing that was hardest was the jealousy, at least for Mary Ann and I. And sometimes it wasn't about, you know, me, but it was just about life. He would love to talk about politics and economics. I never understood all that but I liked to listen to him. I learned a lot."

Mary Ann remembers "one thing that's sort of funny. I don't know if I had this yearning to be alone with them or not, but often when they went to bed I would go into their room to discuss the day and say good-night. I just wanted to be with them for a few minutes. I don't know why I did it. From the time I can remember, I used to do it. I think I was the only one." Their parents *tried* to give them as much time as possible. Dad helped Mary Ann with her homework (and her confidence) and Mom became a Girl Scout leader for her, Patsy, and Cathy. According to Mary Ann, when Mom got upset at things, "She'd just talk to Dad and he always said, 'Oh, don't worry about it.' That was his line. She'd wake up at night and worry about things, but Dad would say, 'Oh, just go back to sleep; it will all work out.' " Sometimes her father's confidence infuriated Mary Ann, for "I didn't think everything would work out."

At this time the Holy Rule of St. Benedict played an important part in the Crowley family. In 1945 Pat's Catholic Action group decided to join one of the "third orders" of lay people associated with religious communities like the Dominicans and Franciscans. They chose the Benedictines and drove one weekend with their wives to Collegeville, Minnesota, and were received into the Oblates of St. Benedict. Pat loved the Benedictine Rule. It was family-oriented, democratic (though it stated clearly that the father was head of the family), humorous, and, well, not very specific. "You didn't have to do anything," according to Patty. Besides, Pat was fond of pointing out, you could "drink unto satiety." In the Crowley household Pat often referred to himself as the abbot and cited Benedict's fifteen-hundred-year-old rule. The abbot was to "make no distinction of persons"; everyone, that is, was to be treated fairly and as an individual. The abbot was to "remember who he is." Mindful of his role, Pat would pause just before midnight every New Year's eve to pray and reflect with his family and their guests on the past year. He would remind them to "remember who they were" by not taking themselves too seriously. His favorite advice from the rule, however, was to take counsel "even from the youngest," and so, at the after-dinner meetings in which plans and problems were discussed, he always made it a point to hear the wisdom of the smallest one present.

"We used to try to get the kids to say their rosary—it was one of our actions—and, oh, they hated it," Patty recalls. "My mother had given me a big statue of the Sacred Heart which was marble and was really pretty bad. It was in the hallway. So we devised ways of taking their minds off it. We'd do silly things. We'd walk around the house saying the rosary, and they'd pick up clothes or something like that." On car trips the children were often treated to (or put through) the lives of St. Francis, St. Benedict, St. Catherine of Siena, St. Thérèse of Lisieux. The most important time, however, was Sunday dinner. The abbot, dressed in suit and tie, would lead a discussion of that morning's Scripture or talk about the doctrine of the Mystical Body. There was a rule at the Crowley table: you never had a private conversation with anybody else, no matter how many were present. All talk was directed through Dad to those with whom you shared your meal.

One day in the fall of 1955, neighbors approached Pat and Patty with the story of a baby girl—their godchild—in need of a home. Police had picked up the girl's mother the previous spring when they found her hitchhiking with her three-day-old child. No one knew who the father was. The baby was handed over to foster parents, but the foster parents now feared they were becoming so attached that it would be impossible to give the child up when the time came. They thought it better to have someone else care for her. Would the Crowleys be willing to do so?

Patty's children were ecstatic at the propsect—a baby at last. But she had her doubts. "I wasn't too crazy about having a baby after eight years. I knew what it was to be up at night. But the kids . . . it was really their doing." Theresa arrived on December 12, 1955. Nine months old, she was the last foster child taken by the Crowleys, and the only one who never left. "She always seemed part of our family because she was little. She really didn't have anything of anybody else."

Theresa's experience was unlike that of Al Augustine, who did have "something of somebody else." Because no court had placed him in their home, Pat and Patty thought he should remain close to his own mother. Though Al grew to be as tall as Pat, to look like him, and even to follow him into the law, he never felt fully at home in the Crowley house—or in his mother's, for that matter. Having "two mothers and a dad" sometimes meant having no mother and no dad. Married now and working for the government, he says his life still comes down to understanding the experience of living in two worlds and to making a choice between them.

"As I look back on my life, and I have many, many times, I always think I was in a unique position. I saw both worlds, more than most young people ever really see. Completely different worlds. I saw the world of love, Christianity, understanding, happiness, activity, wealth; and I saw the world of my mother. She lived in a lot of black neighborhoods. When I used to come home for the summer, I didn't know anybody. And they were all black and I was the little white kid. It didn't make a difference to me because I didn't know any prejudice. The Crowleys didn't train you to be prejudiced. You had blacks to the house, you had green, you had blue, you had everybody. So it didn't make any difference to me, but it did to the black kids, because they wouldn't play with me. So I became the most proficient expert in catching a pop-up in the world, because I'd spend six hours a day running around in the park, throwing a ball up in the air and catching it.

"The biggest switch in my life, and the thing that stunned me the most, was when I learned to hate blacks. They stopped being people and became niggers. That started when I moved to the South Side for the sixth grade. I was the only white player on this little black baseball team. We'd play marbles with the black kids because I'd made friends with a guy by the name of Leonard. That was sixth grade, and by the time I was in seventh grade I wouldn't even talk to Leonard. The kids where I went to school and my mother were a big influence on me. They were all prejudiced. For the first time in my life I learned that blacks were lazy and blacks were immoral and blacks were less than whites and things like that.

"Everybody I knew was Catholic. Both worlds. The people on the South Side were very religious. Very ignorant in their religion but very religious. The Crowleys were very religious, very smart people, but yet, in a lot of ways, very ignorant—in my judgment. I am not religious. I was. I was very, very religious. If you were raised in the Crowley household, you were religious. There were two basics in life up there. One was the family dinner, and Dad would rule over dinner. The other was religion. And then everybody sort of did their own thing after that.

"There wasn't any question about it that Dad was the one you loved and Mom was the one you loved but respected more than you loved. Except if he got mad. And then he'd growl and be tough, but then he'd end up smiling at you. Most people don't think of him as ever getting mad, but he did. He'd blow his top once in a while, but never for very long, and he wouldn't hold a grudge. It wouldn't last for more than half an hour.

"He liked to get along with people rather than have confrontations. He got along with everybody. He had such a good laugh and such a good smile. It was contagious. People around him would start laughing, and pretty soon everybody would be laughing, even though nothing was funny. He was just happy and you felt good around him. You may have disagreed with him but you couldn't not like him.

"I've been through political things with him. I've been through legal things with him. Right after the McCarthy thing in 1968 Dad would see Mayor Daley walking down the street, and the mayor would walk across the street and say hello to him. He liked him, and they were in a bitter political feud.

"Mom was a hard-driving, very organized, very efficient businesswoman. She could run General Motors. Dad used to say that and he was absolutely right. They used to have a joke: Dad would always be very late and Mom would always be on time and therefore they'd be a little late. They worked together perfectly in that way, as two people. They had infinite energy. I tried to stay with them one week and do all they did. I got exhausted. I couldn't make it. They'd go from eight in the morning till ten at night. I couldn't do that—and I was a college kid. Dad would be smiling and bullshitting with people, and Mom would say, 'Come on, let's go, we've got to do this.'

"Mom and Dad tried to take the kids to things as much as they could, and they tried to be around the kids, but I don't think the kids knew them. Except for Patsy. Patsy was the oldest. Dad really had a special relationship with her and maybe she knew him really well. I don't know. I don't think any of the other kids did.

"It's not just a question that they were away. I think it's a question of personality. Patrick and I weren't buddies with our father. We'd do things once in a while, but we weren't friends. He was Dad and you were the son and you loved being with him and you loved having a good time with him, but you didn't get to know him. I never got to know him, you know, the way I know people. I get to know people very easily. He's not easy to get to know. Mom's even harder to get to know. I know we get along. She likes me and I like her. But I would love to get to know her.

"There was a great love, an overwhelming love, but it all made it seem like it was okay, and sometimes it really wasn't okay. And you'd try to explain that and say, 'But it's not okay.' And Dad would say, 'Well, it's all right.' And you'd say, 'Dammit, it's not all right; I've got problems right now.' I remember in college and law school a couple of times writing letters to them. That was the best way for me to talk to them, to put it all out in a letter. And I'd be crying when I was writing the letter, but I'd do it. You couldn't say to Dad, 'Well, let's go out and have a beer, just you and I.' He would do that with Patrick once in a while, but with me not very often. And not with Patrick very much either, really. You didn't do that with him.

"I think they tried. I think they asked the kids to tell them their problems. You could sit down and they'd talk to you. They'd close the door in one room or the other and have some long talks. Dad's reaction to almost all those things was that it's going to work out okay, it's going to be fine. I don't recall very much specific advice. Emotional advice rather than specifics. Assurances and stuff like that and try to calm you down rather than really trying to jump in there and say, 'Let's solve this together.' I don't think the kids felt satisfied all the time with it. I know I didn't. I wanted a little more help in getting an answer. I didn't want it always to be thrown back to me with 'Okay, you figure out the whole thing.' At times of really bad stress, you want somebody to tell you at least what your two alternatives are or sometimes even what to do. And he'd never do that. It wasn't his nature. He wouldn't do that in the law business. He wouldn't do that in any other way that I knew him.

"Mom and Dad could be pushed around incredibly easily. They were taken advantage of all the time. Absolutely all the time. They would draw the line, I guess, at some point but, good Lord . . . . The best example of that is this foreign student from Africa. He had been borrowing money from them for years to finish his education here. And he borrowed more money and more money. Dad would always tell me, 'I can't give that guy any more money. He's just not doing what he should be doing.' And he would call and Dad would say, 'I just gave him some more money. What did I do that for?' He was a pushover. He'd draw the line at some things but as a general rule . . .

"I don't think he was naive. He was too bright for that. I think he knew he was being pushed over. I think he was in his own way powerless to stop it from happening because of something inside of him. I don't know exactly what it was. Maybe he didn't want to be tough and say no or he thought he had some obligation or maybe he did it out of pure love or he thought it was the right thing to do. On certain things he would put down his foot, but that was the exception more than the rule.

"I remember three Cuban students who came to our house right after the Cuban crisis. They were just obnoxious kids. Very spoiled rich kids from Cuba. And they would sit at the dinner table and talk in Spanish. I remember Mary Ann and Cathy and I really got angry. We went and talked to the kids. Told them that 'If you don't stop . . . maybe Mom and Dad won't do anything, but we're going to have them get you out of this house unless you start being a part of this family. Because that's the way we view it, it's one family. And, if you're here, you're part of the family. We'll treat you that way. So don't try to be better, or don't try to separate yourself from it.' And I was enough of the family at that time that I could say that.

"But yet I also wasn't part of the family a lot. When they went on trips, I didn't go. The family went, but I went back to my mother's or I would stay at the house. That was something that hurt me a lot because I didn't understand it as a kid. I think if I were going to do it, I would have done it differently. If I took in a foster child and I had my own children, I think I'd take them on the same trips. But, on the other hand, the Crowleys also had a view, and I'm not saying it's wrong, that their family was very, very important to them, and they knew who the blood family was. They had all the other people and they loved them and they treated them as equal as they could. Up to a point. But there was that point with everybody.

"One time we were going to go horseback riding down in Lincoln Park. I'd gone up to sleep, to rest because I was going to get to go riding, too. I woke up and I walked downstairs and Mom said, 'Oh, did they forget you?' I just went and cried. They had gone. When they got to Evanston, they realized that I wasn't in the car and they called.

Mom drove me down and I went. I'm sure I remember it because I was so horrified that I was going to miss it, and all of a sudden I got to go. I would always feel like I was being left out.

"I'm not going to start getting emotional, because I can on something like that. I remember when I was a senior in high school, and Dad had met the president of YCS at Notre Dame and he was talking about how impressive this guy was. He was really impressed with the young man. Well, I became president four years after that, and I didn't feel like he really . . . I didn't get a positive reaction like, 'That's really good.' I was always doing what I thought they would be proud of, but I never felt they were. They praised the children very much—their kids. Me, not nearly as much. That was the separation between me and them.

"My mother on the South Side was well known and loved by all Lithuanians. I wasn't. When I came to live there, I didn't speak Lithuanian. I was raised with an Irish Catholic family in the suburbs. I wasn't musical. Most Lithuanians are. I mean, I love music and things like that, but I wasn't like she was. My mother was a big-shot Lithuanian. It was her whole life. I was never a part of it.

"The biggest problem was the insecurity that I had in my life. Little by little, as I get older, I become a little less insecure.

"You see both worlds, and if you take time at some point in your life to think about them, you have to make some judgments. You have to make some decisions about what you believe in. I know where I want to go. I like the one world a lot better. I like to be happy. I like not to be poor. I'd rather like people than dislike people. I have rejected the South Side world. I've rejected the ignorance, in my opinion, and the Lithuanian mentality which I am, and was. My group of friends there didn't become professionals. The smartest kids became officers in banks.

"But I still like a lot of things that I had on the South Side. I still do a lot of things with my friends from there. I like bowling as opposed to yachting. I don't like some of the high-falutin' stuff, but then neither did the Crowleys. My mother, unlike the Crowleys, pushed and demanded. She gave me a lot of drive. She was a very tough, tough woman. Came here without a penny and bought a house. She was going to make it.

"The Crowleys had ideas, they had the money behind them, and they had the freedom because of both their families' wealth. They could take all these trips and go around and give all these talks because of their position and their money. If I could deal with my wife and accomplish one-tenth, one-hundredth of what they did, my life would be a tremendous success in terms of accomplishments.

Errata

Acknowledgments page, line 20: *For* Conners *read* Commers

"What I learned from them were mainly intangibles. A sense of morals. That's probably the biggest thing. A sense of trying to do what's right and honest. Not skills. You didn't learn skills around there. I don't think any of the kids are tremendously skillful at anything. But they are all good kids. I think it was more a feeling good, a liking of people.

"Mom and Dad never said, 'I've got it all figured out.' They were always willing to learn. And they changed constantly. I remember when I was in college I got into an argument with Mom one time about canon law. We had this, not a real argument, but a long discussion about it, and she was adamant. Six months later I remember hearing them at a talk somewhere and she was saying exactly what I was saying six months earlier. I looked and I said, 'That's super! You were not so closed in your mind that you couldn't change.'

"It's an interesting dichotomy to see the two different worlds, back and forth, at the same time. It has taught me to understand people. I can understand the executives where I work and get along with them. I can understand the investigators, who are at a lower level, and get along with them. Because I've lived with both of them. They're people. They're just coming from different places, have different backgrounds, and different training and different experiences as kids.

"I always see those two worlds, and I know where I want to go."

Outside the Collegio Spagnolo with Cardinals Dearden of Detroit, Sheehan of Baltimore, and Döpfner of Munich.

CHAPTER NINE
THE BIRTH CONTROL COMMISSION

Greeting Pope Paul VI.

From the U.S.A., Canada, and France came the commission's only three married couples—the Crowleys, the Potvins, and the Rendus. No pictures were allowed of the commission's deliberations. This photo was snapped with a Polaroid after the last session.

Early in December, 1964, a letter of enormous consequence reached the home of the Patrick Crowleys. Signed by the Vatican Secretary of State, A.G. Cicognani, it had come by way of the Apostolic Delegate to the United States and the archbishop of Chicago, Albert Cardinal Meyer. Its contents were brief and direct: "The Holy Father had deigned to appoint you members of the special Committee for studies on problems of population and birth control." Accompanying the letter were the congratulations of Cardinal Meyer and his request that news of the appointment not be made public.

Pat and Patty were stunned. Two decades before, Pat had been one of six "guys" meeting in Chicago's Loop to grope with new ideas about the laity's role in the Church and joke about Pius XII's encyclical about their conversations. At the same time Patty was part of a group of suburban women discovering that there was more to life than parties and that housewives were equipped with brains. Both had been exhilarated in their living-room discussions on the family by nothing more than priests who listened instead of preached. Now came an invitation from the Pope to participate at the highest level in the Church's reflection on its most troubling issue. It seemed the laity, and the women among them, had come a long way indeed.

The committee to which the Crowleys were named was originally a group of six experts appointed by John XXIII to advise him on matters of population and family planning, with special reference to the newly developed birth-control pill. The appointments were made in the spring of 1963, half a year after John opened the Second Vatican Council. At the time, the United Nations was debating the population question and Catholic theologians were beginning to discuss the morality of the pill. John wished to make a fresh examination of the Church's stand against contraception. He died before his advisory group ever met, but his successor, Paul VI, continued to sponsor its activities and even increased its membership. Yet, even after three meetings in a year's time, the predominantly conservative panel could not reach unanimity. In the face of mounting pressure for clarification from Catholics around the globe, Paul would only say a "grave moral problem" was still under study.

On June 23, 1964, Paul formally established his advisory panel as the Special Study Group on Population and Birth Control. He spoke of the urgency of its mission and announced his intention to enlarge it even more. Carefully investigating candidates from all over the world, he brought its membership to fifty-seven. On the reconstituted panel were theologians, economists, demographers, philosophers, and doctors, including psychiatrists, psychologists, and one acupuncturist. There were bishops and priests, but the majority of participants were laity, women being included for the first time. The United States delegation of nine was the largest among the twenty countries represented. The stated purpose of the commission was to make a careful investigation of the matters of population and contraception so the pope, "supported by the light of human science," might ultimately pass judgment on them. Nevertheless, onlookers wondered why a commission would even be established unless a change in the Church's teaching was forthcoming.

Among the fifty-seven delegates were three couples, one from Canada, one from France (both conducted clinics in the rhythm method), and the Crowleys. Though no one realized it at the time, all three wives were incapable of conceiving. There were two single women on the panel, a physician from India and a demographer from the Philippines. The Crowleys were never told why they had been selected, but they surmised it was because of their leadership in CFM, a position that kept them in touch with tens of thousands of families in the United States and throughout the world. Feeling themselves to be the only participants who were not "experts," Pat and Patty decided that their role was to speak for "plain married couples," not just the ones who visited doctors or came to rhythm clinics, and that they had to consult as many of these couples as possible.

When they received that surprising letter from the Vatican, the Crowleys were unquestioning believers in papal infallibility. Their thinking was that of their longtime spiritual guide, Monsignor Hillenbrand. Hillenbrand was a social activist because papal encyclicals called for social activism. He was a staunch opponent of contraception for the same reason: papal teaching was consistent and unequivocal in its opposition to it.

Early in their marriage, the Crowleys themselves had struggled with birth control. In the 1930s and '40s the issue for Catholic couples was not whether one was limited to rhythm for birth regulation but whether one could use rhythm at all. Though he did not explicitly condemn rhythm, Pius XI stated in 1930 that the marital act could not be used to frustrate in any way its "natural power to generate life." In 1951 Pius XII said that, for serious reason, one could confine intercourse to the infertile periods of a woman's cycle. Catholics of the Crowley's generation were caught in the middle. One minute rhythm was a sin, the next minute it wasn't, and most of the time it didn't work anyhow. Pat thought it a nuisance to check the calendar continually, so the Crowleys rarely practiced birth control. Most of their friends did likewise.

But after the birth of their fourth child and Patty's near-death in 1947, the Crowleys were spared the worry of conception. Patty could no longer bear children. While most Catholics struggled with rhythm through the next two decades, the Crowleys found no difficulty complying with the teaching of the Church.

Before the commission's first meeting in March, 1965, Pat and Patty tried to solicit as much opinion as possible. They conferred with Cardinal Meyer, Monsignor Hillenbrand, theologians of their acquaintance, and other Americans on the panel. To get the views of ordinary couples they wrote to the executive committees of CFM in Canada and the United States and talked to as many CFMers as they could. On the way to Rome, they stopped in Dublin to meet with a CFM group and visited two priests from a nearby seminary who were saying that contraception was not intrinsically evil. Between those priests and the couples who had already confided in them, the Crowleys began to wonder about the Church's traditional ban on birth control.

When the two of them arrived at the Collegio Spagnolo, a newly completed seminary on the outskirts of Rome, Pat was assigned a room inside but Patty was informed that she would be staying with the four other women at a nearby convent. Wives would not be sleeping with their husbands. "One way of solving the problem," Pat muttered under his breath. Not only were women forbidden to enter the sleeping quarters of the seminary, three days later they heard themselves addressed by Pope Paul as "Dear Sons."

When the delegates gathered on the eve of the formal meetings, Pat suggested to the assembled experts that they break the ice with a community sing. There were no takers. Undaunted, he proposed they sing at mass the next morning. The commissioners agreed to that, even though their common repertoire was limited to *Tantum Ergo* and *Salve Regina*. Later, when Pat and Patty introduced themselves to the demographer from the Philippines, Miss Conception surprised them by saying, "I already know you. I was a guest at your home seven years ago."

The meetings lasted four days. Delegates attended mass at 7:30 A.M., had breakfast, and then broke into three groups, theologians in one room, doctors and natural scientists in a second room, social scientists in a third. Each participant presented a paper prepared in advance and secretaries kept minutes of the ensuing discussions, which were conducted in French and English. In the afternoon, summaries of the morning's deliberations were presented to the full assembly. There were morning and afternoon coffee breaks, but the formal work did not end until dinner at 8:00 P.M. At the Crowleys' suggestion, the commissioners changed tables at every meal so they would get to know everyone on the panel. The Collegio doors were locked at ten—only after the women had been escorted to the convent.

In the opening sessions delegates were continually asking, "What do *they* want?" *They* seemed to mean some higher power in the Vatican. Only after hours of discussion did the commission begin to feel that *it* was the *they*, that the real question was, "What do *we* want?"

For the most part Pat and Patty listened, attempting to digest a staggering amount of factual information: projections of world population and food production; summaries of laws related to birth control, sterilization, and abortion; data on the effectiveness of known methods of birth control and birth-control programs; explanations of the physiological effects of the pill and the intrauterine device; histories of the Church's teaching on the protection of life and the sanctity of marriage. They discovered that most Indian marriages were still arranged by parents, that the widespread practice of abortion had Japanese economists worrying about a labor shortage, that Africans prized large families as status symbols. They heard theologians argue that contraception was "against nature" and scientists rebut, "What do you mean by nature?"

A substantial impact was made by John Noonan, an American professor of law invited to present the history of the Church's teaching on contraception. Between A.D. 50 and 200, Noonan informed the panel, the meaning of sexuality was a turbulent question in the Church. On the right were those who found in the example of Christ and the emphasis of the Gospels on virginity a commandment that all Christians abstain from sexual intercourse. On the left were Christians who claimed that Christ freed them from the Mosaic Law in such a way that sexual license was part of the liberty of the redeemed. In the center were the great majority of Christians who accepted marriage as an institution but sought a rationale for it. What became the rationale was the Stoic belief that it was proper to engage in sexual intercourse only within marriage and then only for generative purposes. In the course of succeeding centuries this opinion was modified so that the procreative purpose became primary but not exclusive; nonetheless, the Church tied legitimate sexual activity chiefly to generation.

To understand the tenacity with which the Church fathers clung to the rule, Noonan continued, one had to understand the utter disregard for young life in the world encountered by Christians. Infanticide and abortion were common practices. The line between seed and embryo was not as clear then as now; hence, Christian writers, in their desire to protect embryonic life, stressed the sacredness of the process by which life was engendered. Moreover, in a society where women were not the equals of men, wives were often sexually exploited by their husbands. By insisting that sexual organs existed for generation alone, early Christians conferred a revolutionary amount of dignity upon women.

Thus, Noonan concluded, you should not be asking, "Are some acts intrinsically against nature?" Christians have always thought it moral to check and channel nature and in this sense to act "against" it. Rather, you should be asking, "Are the rules once necessary to protect procreation, life, and personal dignity now necessary for the community of Christians?"

After his presentation, Noonan was asked by the American Jesuit John Ford to discuss the parallel between contraception and usury. A champion of the rule forbidding contraception, Ford was stunned to hear the reply. The usury rule, Noonan said, once existed as an absolute prohibition against taking profit on a loan, but it underwent substantial modifications as social circumstances changed and new theological analyses were made. Although the rule changed, the fundamental values incarnated in the rule—justice and charity—were preserved. Noonan indicated the same development could occur in regard to contraception.

The formal presentation of the Crowleys was quite brief. They spoke of CFM, of their special contact with "thousands of apostolic, intelligent young families who by their lives have demonstrated a great love for the Church."

> We understand that when the Church was considering the problem of what to do about reviewing the teaching on usury, the testimony of business people was heard and considered. If there is any parallel between the teaching on usury and the teaching on family limitation, then possibly there is a precedent for the testimony of those most affected by the doctrine.
>
> CFM is known to be a sympathetic setting for large families. Since being told of our appointment and being authorized to consult our contemporaries, we have been shocked into a realization that even the most dedicated, committed Catholic couples are deeply troubled by this problem. We have gathered hundreds of statements from many parts of the United States and Canada and have been overwhelmed by the strong consensus in favor of some change. Most expressed a hope that the positive values in love and marriage would be stressed and that an expanded theology of marriage would be developed.
>
> Most say they think there must be a change in the teaching on birth control. Very few know what this change should be. They are puzzled but hopeful.

After four days of intense deliberation, the commissioners were far from a decision on the pill or any specific contraceptive technique. They had realized, however, that they were no one's mouthpiece, that it was up to them alone to make recommendations. With a new sense of responsibility, they shifted their attention from the pill to the broader question of contraception itself. Impressed by what was *not* known, they made assignments for a future meeting and left behind a small committee to prepare an interim report. The report, eighty-three pages long, was delivered to the Pope by Father Henri de Riedmatten, a Dominican who was executive secretary of the commission. Though its contents were carefully guarded, its tone was thought to be liberal.

The Crowley's assignment for the second meeting was to discover for the pastoral section of the panel how CFM husbands and wives throughout the world were faring with the rhythm method. They enlisted the services of Donald Barrett, a Notre Dame sociologist and fellow commissioner, in preparing a questionnaire for distribution to thousands of key CFM couples. An article about their participation on the birth-control commission appeared in the *St. Anthony Messenger* and with it was a request that readers send the Crowleys their comments on the rhythm method. *Act,* in its prime now, began to run pieces debating birth control, one "Catholics and Contraception," by John Noonan, another a set of ten questions inviting readers' comments. The response was overwhelming. Some insisted the Church was wrong; others declared their adherence to her authority; still others expressed their confusion. For every letter that welcomed the discussion there was a canceled subscription.

In no time at all, the Crowleys themselves were inundated with mail. Correspondents, most of them women, opened themselves up to two people they had never met, unloading burdens they had carried for years:

> We are now using the temperature method at 2 days per month. My local doctor calls it "pot luck." I am on the verge of a nervous breakdown with worry, and my doctor also tells me that it would be unwise to have more children. My husband suffers from colitis, which is a nervous disorder aggravated by continual worry of this immense problem. Total abstinence, is this our only answer? Does the Church approve of this state? If so, we will accept its ruling.
>
> But I have heard whispers that some priests give permission to use the pill for various reasons or another (not just for regulation purposes), but only to a certain few. A mortal sin is grave matter and I can't see who can say it is right for one and not another. The Church's teaching to the single person was purity at all times, save yourself for the married state. Now I find it is not only for the single person but for the married person too. Is sex in marriage a sin? I have come to think this wonderful gift is wrong and sinful. Is it only to be used for the procreation of children, and sleeping with one's husband is an occasion of sin?

> As a father and husband, I can't see how a man could be unfaithful to his wife if he had or could have his sexual life at home whenever they both would desire. This issue is almost too late for us because of our age and sex desires, but consideration should be given to future generations.

I "bend over backwards" to avoid raising false hopes on my husband's part. This sounds ridiculous, but I stiffen at a kiss on the cheek, instantly reminded that I must be discreet. I withdraw in other ways, too, afraid to be an interesting companion, gay or witty, or charming; hesitant about being sympathetic or understanding, almost wishing I could be invisible. At the same time I ask myself if my husband resents being dominated by a calendar, or if he misunderstands my cool behavior. And I wonder why I can't shake off the fear and uncertainty during the rest of the month. Even though we have discussed these problems together, they still bother me. I have limited this opinion strictly to rhythm and its effect upon me in regard to the marriage act. Much more could be said about the effects of this tension upon the children, about my husband's feelings in regard to rhythm, and about the early years of our marriage when we were taught that we have no reason or even right to limit or space our children.

We have a lovely, healthy family and the children are my very life and yet I resent the fact that we have to continue this way for 20 more years. Bills never ending, renting a house with no yard for the children or privacy of our own, putting off medical and dental necessities, etc., and just the terrible fact that I was "embarrassed" to death to be seen pregnant again. What a dread sin to be carrying a child of God, a miracle under my very own heart and not want to shout with happiness to the world that I have been chosen to bear Him another heir. I know this is God's Child as were the last 3 for they were conceived at illogical times and I believe that all that keeps me going at times is the fact that no matter how hard I try, I can't forget "God's Will be done."

Two years ago, a Jesuit visited India, and put many people wise on the Rhythm Method. The couples with whom I have had talks in confidence regarding the use of the rhythm method tend to feel that there is a considerable element of artificiality about it, and the maintenance of temperature charts is much too awkward in the social environment of the average Indian home. Where a number of people live and sleep together in one room, a couple have often to choose a late hour at night or a very early hour at morning—say 1 or 2 A.M.—for the conjugal relationship, at a time when everyone else is fast asleep. All in all, the common attitude among those who know something about the techniques of birth prevention seems to be that the use of the tablet is better than the rhythm method.

I feel the whole situation is basically that of the rights of the child. I am sure that every little one having been created has a right to the love and care of his parents, the right to an education which will fully develop his talents and potential and a right to the time of his parents for correct training. The mental torture undergone by the mother, as in my case, every day until one's period begins or one finds one is pregnant is the other angle. This terrible situation cannot but adversely affect the attitude between husband and wife toward each other, and reflect on the children. The strain while practicing abstinence to establish a pattern soon tells in the general atmosphere of the household. Can this be what God desires? I don't believe it is. I am sure he intends a loving couple to show physical love for each other and make for a really happy and loving atmosphere for the children.

I fully accept and carry out the Church's teachings on this, but I do not believe it to be right. I was greatly relieved when, while carrying my sixth child, I admitted this to myself and I will never again subject myself to shutting out reason and logic which seemed to be pounding at my brains for an honest hearing. Each couple is the minister of their own particular marriage. They alone can decide their capabilities in bringing up a family and in solving their own problems.

My husband is away on long business trips and unfortunately his company doesn't take our calendar into consideration when he has to be gone all over this country and now all over the world. He has left on trips at the wrong time of the month and arrived, all in the same month, at the wrong time of the month.

I think most couples are more than generous with cooperation toward one another in regard to the safe and unsafe periods. However, there are times when it is extremely unfair and certainly has its side effects. Consider the times a couple have been partying and come home relaxed from their cares and feeling that perhaps this old world is not such a bad chore after all, and feeling close and inclined to end their day with the ultimate. The calendar can be a cruel intruder and ends the day often in misery, torment and a great emptiness.

So you see, we are in a great quandary as to what is against nature and what is not. I get a feeling that some of the clergy, since they have no experience in this area, think that we are all filled with overflowing passion that can be released at any time we wish. This just isn't so!

Following my 3rd pregnancy in 2 years I almost smothered the baby with a pillow because I couldn't stand its crying. Now in a few years we will have to abstain entirely, perhaps for years, when I become more irregular due to the menopause. I am very depressed and becoming more so. What will another baby do to me at this age? Mental illness on both sides of my family. I devoutly hope and pray the Council will devise some method, *soon*, more reliable for middle-aged women or at least in time so my girls will not have to go through the years of *unnatural marriage* that we have. I thank God for the understanding husband He send me, but we are both very bitter about the sexual life we have had to lead.

The Rhythm Method worked all right, I felt, until the past year when my periods became very irregular. I finally consulted a Catholic gynecologist who prescribed one of the birth control pills for three months. Diagnosis: hormone imbalance. I was afraid of the pill because I had read of the bad effects it has had on some women, but the doctor insisted it was the best thing he could offer and since we were not living a normal married life—we had already completely abstained for eight months.

I can't begin to tell you the difference the pill made in our relationship within a week. Never before in our married life had either of us felt so free about our sexual love. We became immediately more physically affectionate *outside* of the marital act. We became more communicative, there was a greater feeling of family, we became less critical and less nagging about small everyday things, happier with our particular places in the world. My husband became *more male;* I became *more female;* whereas, we both had begun to feel sort of neuter gender—feelings *we* hadn't even realized we'd lost until we felt them again.

I think the whole birth-control issue has become a matter of politics in the Church—a power struggle between the Traditionalists who fear losing their authority and the forward-thinking people who are not afraid to look at a new concept. The honest truth-seeking Catholic couples are the ones who are caught in the middle; I thoroughly resent being a pawn, where our entire life will be determined by others. We all wish to do what is God's will and to follow our own right conscience, but at the same time, too many of us are afraid to think for ourselves—all we can do is hope and pray that the Holy Spirit will guide those on the Commission to unfailingly search their hearts and minds and find the TRUTH.

Most of the letter writers and questionnaire respondents were in their early thirties and had, on the average, five children. They were anything but the "ordinary" Catholics the Crowleys first imagined them to be. Compared with American Catholics at large, they were far more loyal to Church teaching. (At the time of the Crowley survey half of America's Catholic women under 45 were using some unapproved form of conception control.) And compared with the women being interviewed by panel members at rhythm clinics in Canada and France, their use of rhythm was far less sophisticated and their suffering, consequently, far greater. Their dedication to the Church—and the cost of that dedication—was evident in every line of their replies.

Shaken by what they were reading, Pat and Patty sent copies of letters to the commission secretary in the hope that they would eventually reach the pope. They called upon other delegates in the United States and Canada to go through responses with them. André Hellegers, a commission member and gynecologist from Johns Hopkins University, urged them to send a second questionnaire to CFM contact couples for *random* distribution to CFM members in their dioceses. Hellegers feared the initial data could be attacked as being insufficiently representative. To the question, "What should the Church do?" 78 percent of those in the second survey said, "Change."

In the meantime, liberals on the birth control commission were charging that conservative Vatican officials like Cardinals Ottaviani and Cicognani were trying to undermine their work. Some complained that conservative delegates had been lobbying in the offices of the pope and that the reforming intent of the commission had been diluted in the translation of texts. They wondered when—even if—the commission would meet again.

Paul himself was vacillating. In October of 1965 he addressed the United Nations in New York and described artificial birth control as "irrational." Later that autumn he sent to a Vatican Council group working on marriage a set of recommendations that would have reaffirmed the anticontraception stand of Pius XI's directive, *Casti Connubii*. He seemed to be sidestepping his own commission. But when Father de Riedmatten, Léon-Joseph Cardinal Suenens, and other liberals protested, he reconsidered, saying his recommendations were not meant to be definitive. In its closing session the Council ratified a scheme on "The Church in the Modern World" that advised Catholics to avoid methods of birth control found blameworthy by the Church, but left open the question of precisely what was blameworthy. The matter was back in the hands of the papal commission.

The delegates finally reconvened in the spring of 1966. Theologians began work on April 18. The Crowleys were present for a week in May and another in June. They decided it was Patty's place to speak for the large number of women who had written of their experiences with rhythm, so after the reports of their surveys were circulated she presented the commissioners with "A Woman's Viewpoint":

> During our adult lives we have worked with married people. We have talked with them, argued with them, perhaps preached to them more than we like to recognize, worked with them, and, most important, we have listened to them. Our work in the Christian Family Movement, which is now active in sixty-one countries, has taken us around the world several times. Just last month we visited CFM people in Australia, New Zealand, South Africa, Nigeria, Uganda, Tanzania. Since our appointment to this Commission we have asked people how they feel about these momentous questions. We have asked them informally, in casual conservation—where so much can be said in so few words—and we have asked them in three, formal, scientific surveys. So we think that we can speak with some authority on how the married people we know and work with feel. Let me summarize a few of our conclusions.
>
> *Is there a bad psychological effect in the use of rhythm?* Almost without exception, the responses were that, yes, there is.

Does rhythm serve any useful purpose at all? A few say it may be useful for developing discipline. Nobody says that it fosters married love.

Does it contribute to married unity? No. That is the inescapable conclusion of the reports we have received. In marriage a husband and wife pledge themselves to become one in mind, heart, and affection. They are no longer two, but one flesh. Some wonder whether God would have us cultivate such unity by using what seems to them an unnatural system.

I must add that the best place for children to learn the importance of love is from the example of their parents. Yet these reports seem to indicate that instead of unity and love, rhythm tends to substitute tension, dissatisfaction, frustration, and disunity.

I feel that I would be disloyal to women if I didn't also emphasize one other point: We have heard some men, married and celibate, argue that rhythm is a way to develop love. But we have heard few women who agree with them.

Is rhythm unnatural? Yes—that's the conclusion of these reports. Over and over, directly and indirectly, men and women—and perhaps especially women voice the conviction that the physical and psychological implications of rhythm are not adequately understood by the male Church. Over and over, respondents point out that nature prepares a woman at the time of ovulation to have the greatest urge to mate with her husband. Similarly at that time, her husband wants to respond to his wife. She craves his love. Yet month after month she must say no to her husband because it is the wrong date on the calendar or the thermometer reading isn't right.

No amount of theory by men will convince women that this way of making and expressing love is natural.

Notice how the reactions in our report contradict what in the past has been the stereotyped, conventional way of looking at the Catholic husband and wife and their large family. These fathers and mothers, surveying their children, do not sit back with pride and satisfaction. Instead, they reflect a hardly muted bitterness at a condition in their lives that has forced them to stay apart from each other when their natures cried out for each other.

We think it is time for a change. We think it is time that this Commission recommend that the sacredness of conjugal love not be violated by thermometers and calendars. Marital union does lead to fruitfulness, psychologically as well as physically. Couples want children and will have them generously and love them and cherish them. We do not need the impetus of legislation to procreate—it is the very instinct of life, love and sexuality. It is in fact largely our very love for children as parents and our desire for their full development as committed Christians that leads us to realize that numbers alone and the large size of a family is by no means a Christian ideal unless parents can truly be concerned about and capable of nurturing a high *quality* of Christian life.

Patty's fresh and patently sincere report had a strong impact on the theologians. The impact was augmented by the personal statement of Canadian Colette Potvin, heard in utter silence, on the role of intercourse in the presence of sterility. The day after intercourse, she said, she is reassured about her value as a person, kinder to her children, and a better teacher of them. Sterile procreationally, her intercourse is fertile educationally and thus fulfills one of the primary ends of marriage.

The Crowleys were encouraged to discover that theologians, advancing on the problem by an altogether different road, were nearing the same destination as themselves. In the year between the meetings some had concluded that the old rule was not absolute. Others who were wavering now began to favor change. With hopes rising, Pat and Patty urged that a modification of the Church's positions be part of a comprehensive, positive statement on the values of family life.

The Crowleys left a copy of their report with the assembled delegates and another with the pope himself and then set off on a tour of Europe with three of their children. When they returned to Rome in June, Paul's advisory panel did in fact recommend reform. Votes had been taken by theologians and bishops as to (1) whether contraception was intrinsically evil and (2) whether *Casti Connubii* was irreformable. The results of the balloting and the commission's final report, both carefully guarded secrets, were presented to the pope by Cardinal Julius Döpfner on June 28, 1966. Among the wealth of materials were two brief documents presenting the best arguments for and against reform. Written in a single night by a handful of people on each side, they came to be known as the majority and minority reports.

Both focused on the teaching authority of the Church. In the opinion of the minority, statements against contraception were part of the Church's unchangeable doctrine. "The Church could not have erred through so many centuries, even through one century, by imposing under serious obligation very grave burdens in the name of Jesus Christ, if Jesus Christ did not actually impose these burdens . . . Therefore, one must very cautiously inquire whether the change which is proposed would not bring along with it a definitive depreciation of the teaching and moral direction of the hierarchy of the Church and whether several very grave doubts would not be opened up about the very history of Christianity."[1]

The majority opinion, on the other hand, said that the condemnation of birth control in *Casti Connubii* was not infallible Catholic teaching. The tradition leading to that encyclical was not of apostolic origin nor was it an expression of universal faith. "Sacred Scripture says not only 'increase and multiply,' but 'they shall be two in one flesh.' "[2] According to the majority, humanity had a right, and even a duty, to intervene in nature and shape it to good purposes. That right extended to one's reproductive processes. It was far more in keeping with men and women's rational nature to control conception than to leave it wholly to chance. As to the method of doing so, that was up to the conscience of individual couples.

The Crowleys left Rome thinking the matter was settled, grateful for having had the opportunity to participate in a historic reformation of doctrine. They thought the pope was compelled by the size of the majority to ratify the panel's advice. Still pledged to secrecy, they told only Monsignor Hillenbrand what had taken place. Unimpressed, he said, "We'll wait to see what the pope says."

A year passed and nothing came from Rome, no statement from the pope, no word from fellow commissioners. In April 1967, a commissioner leaked to *Le Monde* in Paris and the *National Catholic Reporter* in the United States copies of the majority and minority reports. It was an apparent attempt to force the Pope's hand. What had been suspected by the press was now confirmed for Catholics throughout the world: Paul VI's own study group had said that birth control was not evil and that the Church's teaching could be changed.

Statistics later showed that American Catholics by this time had decided for themselves to accept the pill and to do so with a clear conscience. Pill-users, in fact, received communion more frequently than rhythm-users. In the fall of 1967 Pat and Patty surveyed one thousand CFMers—a very select group of American Catholics—and found the same thing. Eighty-one percent now felt that "in the end, the person has to make his decision with God alone." Some CFM couples already were practicing unapproved methods of birth regulation. Ten percent of the respondents were doing so *and* frequenting the sacraments.

On the chance that they could move Rome in a favorable direction, Pat and John Noonan decided to have a conference for a small number of "high-level papal people," including some who served on the commission. They obtained from the Rockefeller Foundation a small grant and the use of its Villa Serbelloni on Lake Como in Italy. Invitations were extended to twenty-five bishops, theologians, and laity for a conference in June, 1968, on "Education for Responsibility and Love in Marriage." The invitations were accepted, but as June approached, something curious happened. One by one, the bishops—even the liberal Cardinal Suenens—began to send their regrets. The meeting had to be postponed.

Rumors spread in June that Paul was going to promulgate a document in opposition to the commission's recommendation. He held off when liberal prelates who previewed the text reacted vigorously. At the end of that month he issued "The Credo of the People of God," a forceful restatement of general Catholic teaching that left untouched the matter of birth control, but was very clear about papal infallibility. Though the pope had not reacted in an official capacity to the commission's work, the signs were far from propitious.

Then, at four o'clock in the morning of July 29, 1968, the Crowleys were awakened by the telephone. A newspaper was calling to get their reaction to the encyclical. They knew of no encyclical and so were told the shocking news: Paul VI had promulgated *Humanae Vitae*, a document that rejected the advice of the birth-control panel and reasserted the Church's ban against contraception. Half asleep, Pat expressed his amazement and disappointment and then hung up.

Within a week he and his wife endorsed a statement of two hundred Catholic scholars that took exception to the encyclical. "History shows that a number of statements of similar or even greater authoritative weight have subsequently been proven inadequate or even erroneous," the scholars said. "We conclude that spouses may responsibly decide according to their conscience that artificial contraception in some circumstances is permissible and indeed necessary to preserve and foster the values and sacredness of marriage."[3] They were joined by John Noonan, André Hellegers, and the three other American laymen on the commission. A few days later the Crowleys and eighteen other United States delegates to the 1967 World Congress of the Laity affirmed a similar position.

The Crowley's subsequent remarks to the press were respectul of Church authority but clear in their opposition on this issue. Pat told the *National Catholic Reporter* that *Humanae Vitae* "represents a very heroic opinion of the Pope but I don't think it binds anybody to stop thinking about it or talking about it."[4] Patty told the *Chicago Sun-Times* that Catholics should take their cue from Vatican II's statements on marriage and the family rather than from the encyclical.[5] She amplified for the *National Register*: "There's a negative element about the encyclical which reflects a negative approach to the concept of marriage itself—and this in spite of the positive and hopeful approach taken in the Vatican II documents. . . . Trained and educated younger couples will not forget that sense of responsibility given them by the Council Fathers, and will maintain that the problem is one for solution by their own consciences."[6]

Their public dissent brought angry letters from a few CFM couples. To these Pat responded with gentleness but without backing off from his position. Their stance also cost them the support of Chicago's highest ranking prelate and the friendship of the man who had been their inspiration for twenty-five years. "Cardinal Cody has never talked to us and neither has Monsignor Hillenbrand," Patty relates. Cody came to Chicago when Cardinal Meyer died in 1965 and gradually chilled the climate in which CFM and other Catholic Action efforts had thrived. Hillenbrand severely reprimanded the Crowleys for their response to *Humanae Vitae*. Patty was deeply hurt and never went back to talk to him.

Pat felt that discussion of the birth-control issue should continue, but soon discovered that people were not in the mood for discussion. In the fall of 1968 he sent yet another survey to contact couples in the International CFM, but the response—a deluge three years before—was only a trickle. The tenor was different, too. Gone was the moral anguish over the principle of birth control and in its place was uncertainty over the side effects of the pill.

To Patty, *Humanae Vitae* was a sudden, unprovoked blow, coming when years of work, absolutely voluntary and carried out with the sincerest intentions, seemed on the verge of success. Her faith in the Church suffered in the aftermath of the pope's action. She had made a personal cause of forcing the Vatican to hear the anguished cries of thousands of its most loyal women, women who had entrusted to her and Pat the intimate details of their lives. In 1966 relief for her correspondents seemed assured, but in 1968 it was suddenly withdrawn. "We realized afterward that a small minority had stayed in Rome and worked on the pope," she says. "We never heard a word from Rome since. It's a funny thing: nobody who was on the commission wanted to talk about it afterward. The people we knew in the States became disillusioned."

Pat, on the other hand, seemed incapable of disenchantment. *Humanae Vitae* was the first of a series of setbacks that anyone else would have called tragedies. Some inner corner of him may have struggled with the encyclical, or despaired at the waste of so much effort, or even had a premonition of the reversals the encyclical would bring to CFM. But all who knew Pat looked on with amazement as his spirit did what it always seemed to do: dance on with the confidence that no matter how bad things looked now, in the end all would be well. While Pat disagreed with the papal directive, he could not understand why anyone would leave the Church because of it. "Their faith couldn't have amounted to much in the first place," he said on one occasion, and besides, "there are *other* issues facing the world and the Church."

One of those issues, absorbing his energy at the time *Humanae Vitae* appeared, further foreclosed the possibility of despair. The Crowleys had moved to an apartment on Chicago's Near North Side; a presidential candidate who charged gaily at the impossible had enlisted Pat's support; and the city was nervously awaiting the 1968 Democratic National Convention.

CHAPTER TEN
McCARTHY FOR PRESIDENT

Scenes from the 1968 campaign. Cathy is at the lower right.

Gathering in Chicago.

One of the promises Marietta Caron extracted from Pat when he asked for the hand of her daughter in 1937 was that he never enter politics. Marietta regarded politicians, especially those of the Democratic species, about as favorable as she did Irishmen. Though Pat kept his promise, at least the letter of it, for many years, in 1968 he and his family became as involved in politics as one can be without actually running for office.

Politics had a history in the Crowley family, but it had usually been the politics of the G.O.P. Pat's father was a Republican but his mother and his beloved Uncle George were Democrats. George Crowley, in fact, was an active politician who held various offices in the party's Cook County organization. He often discussed politics within earshot of his nephews and may have been the one who arranged for Pat, then sixteen, to attend the 1928 Democratic convention which nominated Al Smith for president.

Pat worked for Smith and saw him lose to Herbert Hoover. In 1932, in the fall of his senior year at Notre Dame, Pat turned twenty-one and voted like his father for the Republican candidate. This time, however, Hoover was repudiated by a country reeling from the depression, and the victory went to Franklin Roosevelt. Pat's social conscience suddenly came alive. Like many young people of his time, he was caught up in the excitement and hope of Roosevelt's first one hundred days. As the president unfolded his New Deal over the radio, Pat studied the ideas of John Ryan on distributive justice. Slowly he edged to the political center and then to the left of center. By the time he graduated in June 1933, he had been drawn by Ryan and Roosevelt to the side of the Democrats. His father had made exactly the same journey.

Pat made no extraordinary political effort for more than twenty-five years, save for an occasional intervention in local government—usually a CFM action. But when John Kennedy was nominated in 1960, Pat and Patty, now a Democrat herself, went to work with vigor. Patty helped start a Democratic Women's Club in Republican Wilmette and with the few other Democrats in town sent out entire families to canvass for Kennedy. It was an encouraging initiation to campaigning. Not only did Kennedy upset Nixon in Wilmette, he also carried the country at large. The Crowleys threw a huge celebration party, and Pat wasted no time inviting the president and his family to the CFM convention the following August. He knew the chances were slim that Kennedy would address a Catholic gathering so early in his presidency, but Pat never hesitated before the impossible. This time the impossible proved precisely that: White House secretaries sent the president's regrets.

Three years after his election, Kennedy was mortally wounded in the streets of Dallas. Four years later, on November 30, 1967, Minnesota Senator Eugene McCarthy startled the nation by announcing that he would seek the Democratic nomination for president, challenging Kennedy's successor on a single issue: peace in Vietnam. The war and Lyndon Johnson, said McCarthy, had to be opposed as a matter of conscience.

Few observers thought McCarthy had the slightest chance of unseating the president. Most thought he was either committing political suicide or harmlessly tilting at windmills. In January, 1968, public and private polls estimated McCarthy's share of the vote in the upcoming New Hampshire primary at about 10 percent. New Hampshire was a "hawkish" state; its defense-related industries thrived during the war while few of its men were being killed. From all appearances it was a poor place for McCarthy's first confrontation with the president.

What the polls and the pundits failed to foresee was the avalanche of students—the "children's crusade"—that poured into snowy New Hampshire in February and March to volunteer their services for the antiwar candidate. Thousands hitchhiked or chartered buses from as far away as Washington and Baltimore to stuff envelopes, make phone calls, and knock on doors for "Clean" Gene McCarthy. On March 12, 1968, the Democratic voters of New Hampshire shook the political world by giving McCarthy 42 percent of their votes, compared with Johnson's 49 percent. When write-in votes from Republicans were added in, the two candidates were nearly neck-and-neck, Johnson drawing 29,021 to McCarthy's 28,791. The candidate of peace was on his way.

Pat Crowley had been called by McCarthy's office during the last hectic weeks of the New Hampshire campaign. Patty is unaware of the details of the communication except that Pat was elated by it and immediately sent in a contribution. Pat had met McCarthy at the 1959 CFM convention, at which McCarthy was the principal speaker. After New Hampshire showed that he was a candidate to be reckoned with, Pat received another call. Would he join the senator's campaign in Illinois? The Crowleys' organizational ability, their fund-raising skills, their connections with Chicago politicians, their influence within the CFM network, all recommended them strongly to McCarthy. Pat's response was an immediate yes. He scheduled a thousand-dollar-a-head cocktail party for March 27 and then drove to Milwaukee to join McCarthy.

The McCarthy forces in Wisconsin were still euphoric over New Hampshire but nonetheless worried about Bobby Kennedy's entry into the race. (Kennedy announced his candidacy on March 16.) Driving themselves hard on the friendly terrain of the dairy state, they hoped for a stunning victory over the president. But on March 31, two days before the primary, Lyndon Johnson appeared on national television to declare a bombing halt over North Vietnam. He concluded his speech with a historic sentence: "I shall not seek and I will not accept the nomination of my party for another term as your president." The election results two days later was academic: McCarthy 56 percent of the Democratic vote, Johnson 35 percent.

It had been easier to topple the president than anyone had anticipated.

Two days after the Wisconsin primary, another assassin's bullet killed Martin Luther King, Jr., and cities, Chicago among them, exploded in violence. The horror was repeated June 4 at a victory celebration in Bobby Kennedy's California headquarters. After defeating McCarthy in Indiana and Nebraska and losing to him in Oregon, Kennedy had won convincingly in their most important showdown to date. Rousing his supporters with "On to Chicago," he had left the ballroom of Los Angeles's Hotel Ambassador, exiting by way of the kitchen, and walked into the ambush of Sirhan Sirhan.

A renunciation and now an assassination had narrowed the agonizing Democratic race to McCarthy and Vice-President Hubert Humphrey, who had announced his candidacy on April 27. The nation's emotions were being rubbed raw.

Most of the Crowley family concentrated that summer on working for McCarthy. Since voters in the 1968 Illinois primary did no more than select delegates to the convention, the campaign first tried to elect candidates pledged to McCarthy. On June 11, however, McCarthy delegates were swamped by the uncommitted slate controlled by Chicago Mayor Richard Daley. The victories of two McCarthy supporters, neither from the Chicago area, prevented a total whitewash. After the primary, McCarthyites in Illinois tried to convince Daley and his 115 "uncommitted" delegates that their candidate had the broad popular support that Humphrey lacked. It was not easy. Daley had supported Bobby Kennedy, then Humphrey, and in July endorsed the idea of drafting Teddy Kennedy. Of all the candidates it was McCarthy to whom he was coolest.

On June 30 a quarter of a million dollars was raised at a rally featuring Peter, Paul and Mary, Cleveland Amory, Dick Benjamin, Paula Prentiss, and McCarthy himself. The following weekend was for the less affluent. Young people all over the state were asked to "Clean for Gene"—to wash cars, mow lawns, clean houses, wash windows, and send the proceeds to McCarthy. (In New Hampshire "Clean for Gene" meant you got a haircut and shaved before you canvassed for him.) At a press conference on July 9 it was announced that Pat Crowley had assumed chairmanship of the McCarthy campaign in Illinois. Pat immediately directed McCarthy backers to flood the mayor—at his home, not at City Hall—with letters and lists of signatures in support of their candidate. Pat said he was not harassing Daley, simply demonstrating McCarthy's strength among the electorate. He noted that Humphrey may have been ahead in delegate strength but he wasn't drawing the crowds or winning the battles of the polls.

Pat and Patty proceeded to manage the campaign the way they managed CFM. He lit up with ideas, spoke, and wrote. She organized. Working at headquarters on the eleventh floor of an old building at 22 W. Monroe, Patty coordinated staff meetings, supervised the dissemination of newsletters, ads, and press releases, directed the distribution of literature, buttons, and bumper stickers, and kept detailed records of expenses and contributions. She offered celebrities like Dustin Hoffman and Tony Randall to anyone who would throw a cocktail party for potential donors to McCarthy's coffers. If a cocktail party was beyond someone's means, she suggested a luncheon, an art sale, or a coffee klatch. The ideas were numerous. Trying to bring some of them about, Patty bristled whenever the national campaign invaded her territory and spent her hard-earned money. McCarthy's workers were every bit as unprofessional as people said.

The Crowley children helped where they could, Mary Ann and Theresa in Chicago, Cathy in both Chicago and the Watts district of Los Angeles, a fruitless desert for McCarthy. They were dazzled by celebrities like Harry Belafonte, Donna Reed, Julian Bond, and John Kenneth Galbraith, who appeared at the Crowley's home for fundraisers exposing McCarthy to influential Chicagoans. When gum-chewing Paul Newman appeared at a cocktail party and asked for a beer, Cathy was stunned to discover that nothing so lowbrow had been stocked. Frantic, she went downstairs to a neighbor, and in no time her idol had several sixpacks at his disposal. (Her mother was never as accommodating to celebrities. In 1972, "M A S H's" Alan Alda came through and asked if he could eat before the other guests. Unwilling to spoil her carefully set table, Patty sent him to the kitchen.)

As the convention drew near, storefronts were set up in swing districts to organize canvassing efforts to gather more signatures for McCarthy. Patty chaired a hospitality committee that attempted to find housing for out-of-town McCarthy volunteers, to provide transportation (by people wearing McCarthy buttons) for all the convention's delegates, and to offer delights like a champagne cruise on Lake Michigan. The committee eventually set up shop in the Conrad Hilton hotel, site of both the McCarthy and Humphrey suites.

The emotions of the entire summer peaked in the last week of August. On two occasions Pat had arranged a meeting between McCarthy and Mayor Daley, but both times McCarthy had canceled. Having listened to endless associates tell him the cause was hopeless, Pat commented at a breakfast meeting that if McCarthy did not get the nomination, he, Pat, would push him for pope. The city of Chicago was not so lighthearted. Knowing that an invasion of young people—McCarthyites, Yippies, radicals, onlookers—was on its way, it worried that the summer's violence would erupt again. The International Amphitheater, site of the convention, was surrounded by a seven-foot-high chain-link fence topped with three strands of barbed wire. Police, riot squads, National Guardsmen, FBI and Secret Service, regular army troops were all on alert. Where would the young people stay? A number of influential Chicagoans, among them Pat Crowley, urged Daley to give them the parks. It wouldn't hurt, Pat said, to let them have a place like Soldiers' Field. But Daley said no. On the Thursday before the convention the police cleared demonstrators out of Lincoln Park. A Yippie fired a shot at them. They fired back and killed him.

On the following Monday, August 26, at 7:30 P.M., the convention opened. Those who counted delegates gave Humphrey between 1,400 and 1,500 and McCarthy between 500 and 600. Since only 1,312 were needed to win, it appeared that all Humphrey had to do was keep his delegates in line and counter any last-minute attempts to draft Teddy Kennedy. McCarthy was not a serious threat. His only hope was to focus enough anti-Humphrey sentiment to prevent a first-ballot victory.

Mary Ann and Cathy were the only Crowleys to get into the convention that evening. Tickets to Convention Hall were scarce, but the two of them managed to get a job with Western Union. As the delegates fought over rules and credentials, centering their debate on the Georgia delegation, Cathy, covered with McCarthy buttons, delivered messages on the floor. The floor was far more interesting than the Western Union desk, so she lingered—too long to suit her employers, who fired her on the spot. They forgot to reclaim her pass, however, which enabled her to return later. The first session ended at 2:45 in the morning with little settled.

On Tuesday, Knight newspapers printed McCarthy's remark that his chances for the nomination were zero. Now Kennedy seemed the only man capable of challenging Humphrey. That evening, amid the continuing debate over credentials, the New York and California delegations waved "We Want Kennedy" banners and tried to enlist additional support. Reports of demonstrations in downtown Chicago, of riots and police clashes in Lincoln Park, filtered into the convention. By midnight the idea of a Kennedy draft had come and gone. By one o'clock peace delegates were shouting that debate on Vietnam was being buried. Others were clapping and chanting, "Let's go home." Mayor Daley gave Chairman Carl Albert the signal to cut. A vote to adjourn ended the second day.

On Wednesday evening the drama was set not in Convention Hall, where Humphrey was eventually nominated on the first ballot, but in the streets of Chicago. Several thousand young people marched down Michigan Avenue toward a waiting line of police, who had determined the marchers would not reach the Hilton Hotel. The police charged, and television cameras allowed the world to see police clubbing people, throwing gas grenades, and dragging limp bodies into paddy wagons.

McCarthy had obtained convention tickets for the Crowleys that morning so they were at his headquarters in the amphitheater when those pictures first came over the air. Patty has never forgotten. "We both got terribly upset. I said to Pat, 'You've got to stop that! You can't let Daley sit at this convention with kids being killed down at the Hilton!' We were so worried about those kids. Twenty of them were living at our apartment. So Pat got somebody's badge and tried to get on the floor to get to Daley, to tell Daley what was happening down there and that he had to stop it.

"I stayed outside and I saw Julian Bond. I said, 'You know what's happening? You've got to do something! You've got to get the delegations to stop the convention!' Well, of course, that was a big joke. To stop the convention over anything was unheard of. But I remember walking with Julian Bond into the California delegation, trying to get them to go in and do something before something happened.

"We couldn't get back to the Hilton—the police wouldn't let us—but we got back to our apartment. We got all the kids back to our apartment safely. We were so worried that half of them would be in jail. We spent the whole night talking to those kids. They were from all over the country—great, great people. Pat was marvelous with them, calming them down and trying to help them understand what was happening. A lot of their friends had been put in jail, and they just couldn't understand why the police were like that. The McCarthy kids were so enthusiastic, but they were mixed up with all the others, the ones who were the ringleaders.

"So the next morning we did go down and tried to help the kids that were in jail. Somebody took up a collection to get some girl—one of the big McCarthy people, a black girl—out of jail. They had bags of pennies and nickels and quarters. Pat and I—it was crazy—we took the car and went to the jail to try to get this girl out of jail with all this money. She wasn't there when we got there. She'd been put in another jail. We spent about three hours at that jail, holding on to the bags of money. The Pat went down to the jail on 18th Street. Some of the police knew him and let him in. All the kids would say, 'Hello, Pat.' They all knew him from events we'd had. And he got her out of jail."

Amid incidents like these the McCarthy campaign of 1968 came to a sudden, devastating conclusion. McCarthy had witnessed the tragedy in the streets Wednesday night from his suite on the 23rd floor of the Hilton. As bloodied demonstrators staggered into the hotel, he and his youthful staff had come to their assistance, tearing up sheets and pillowcases for bandages. Above them, on the 25th floor, Hubert Humphrey was watching the television networks interrupt speeches placing his name in nomination with scenes from the streets. Angered that Humphrey said nothing about the violence, McCarthy refused to appear with him after his acceptance speech at the closing session on Thursday night.

Early Friday morning, police complained of objects being thrown from the Hilton's windows and invaded McCarthy's operational base on the 15th floor. McCarthy appeared in time to prevent them from assaulting and jailing more of his workers and then delayed his own departure from Chicago until that afternoon when he was sure the students were safely on their way. He had seen his workers being beaten and had not heard a word from Humphrey condemning the brutality. He refused to endorse his party's nominee for president, stating that he would concentrate on electing antiwar candidates to the Senate, even if they were Republicans. Eventually he would support Humphrey, but on that Friday newspapers carried his words, "I will not compromise."

Humphrey made up most of the ground lost by the Chicago debacle, but in November was still edged out by Richard Nixon. For the Crowleys, the failure of McCarthy to gain the nomination and Chicago's late-August violence were further disappointments in the wake of the pope's condemnation of birth control. Pat, characteristically, lost little faith in politics—and none in McCarthy—but Patty and especially Cathy were dispirited. In Patty's view, the most tragic aspect of the convention was the disillusioning effect it had on her children, who had loved that summer and were very proud of what their parents had done, and on the student workers to whom they had drawn close.

The Crowleys did not abandon politics, however. In 1972 McCarthy decided to run again and to make Illinois the scene of his first major effort in the primaries. Hoping that Illinois would be his New Hampshire of four years earlier, he asked Pat to chair a $300,000 campaign targeted on the March 21 election.

For the major contenders in '72, Illinois was no more than a whistle-stop between Florida's primary on March 14 and Wisconsin's on April 4. Going into Florida, Edmund Muskie was the front-runner but he won only 9 percent of the Florida vote and finished fourth among eleven candidates. The winner in Florida, one of many states angry over a federal judge's decision to bus children across school districts to achieve racial balance, was George Wallace with 42 percent of the vote. Wallace would continue in the primaries to pound away at "busin' and bureaucrats" until he was shot and crippled at a May rally in Maryland. Hubert Humphrey, Henry "Scoop" Jackson, and John Lindsay all made poor showings in Florida, finishing second, third, and fifth, respectively. Though George McGovern finished sixth with only 6 percent, he accomplished his objective of reducing the far-left tally of Mayor Lindsay. Eugene McCarthy was hardly heard from, finishing eighth with less than 1 percent of the vote.

Most of the candidates bypassed Illinois for a showdown in Wisconsin. Only McCarthy and Muskie entered that primary and both ran hard. Pat and Patty even rented a plane one day and barnstormed the state, stopping in half-a-dozen places, meeting the press, and delivering McCarthy's standard speech. But their efforts were in vain. On March 21, Illinois gave Muskie 63 percent to McCarthy's 37 in a preferential poll and provided him an even greater edge in delegates. Much of McCarthy's total was interpreted as a stop-Muskie effort by voters whose own candidates were not on the ballot. For Muskie it was a last gasp before he lost his wind and faded from the lead. For McCarthy, even for a supporter as enthusiastic as Pat Crowley, it was confirmation that he was going nowhere in '72.

In Wisconsin the tide turned to McGovern, heir to the forces stirred by McCarthy in '68. Unlike McCarthy, however, McGovern surged ahead after Wisconsin and maintained his lead all the way to the July 10 convention in Miami. He had corralled just enough delegates for a first-ballot win, when suddenly he was victimized by a last-minute ambush staged by Hubert Humphrey.

The raid took place in the Credentials Committee of the Democratic party ten days before the convention opened. The committee ruled that 151 of California's 271 delegates, all of them pledged to McGovern, were ineligible and therefore could not be seated. Humphrey supporters had argued that California's unit rule, although legally constituted by that state, violated the guidelines of the party's recent Reform Commission. McGovern had won the California primary with 44 percent of the vote. Although he was entitled to all 271 delegates under California's winner-take-all format, the committee decided he was entitled to only 44 percent, or 120, of the delegates. The 151 vote difference was expected to be his margin of victory.

In retaliation, McGovern backers succeeded in passing a second ruling: Chicago's contingent of 59 "uncommitted" delegates, led by Mayor Daley, were not to be seated with the Illinois delegation. Although the slate of 59 had been elected by 900,000 Cook County voters in the March 21 primary, a rival delegation led by Chicago alderman William Singer charged that it violated reform guidelines because it had been drawn up privately by Daley before the election and because it did not contain a proper mix of women, blacks, Latinos, and youth. Singer's delegation had been elected by no one but itself, but it did comply to the letter with reform rules in its balance of minority representatives, nearly all of whom happened to support McGovern. Listed as alternates on the Singer contingent were a handful of McCarthyites, among them Patty and Cathy Crowley and Al Augustine.

Singer had called Patty after the Illinois primary to ask if she would affix her name to a protest of the "Daley 59" to be lodged with the national Credentials Committee. At the time Patty was unaware that Singer was stacking his slate with McGovernites; he simply said he wanted some McCarthy backers among the challengers. Pat, director of the McCarthy campaign in Illinois, wouldn't do; he was white, male, and sixty. But Patty, a woman, would. "So I talked it over with Pat and I guess he decided it was all right, and I thought, well, it would be fun. I couldn't stand Daley anyway. He had too much power. I felt the challenge was right because of the way they chose delegations at that time—it was all what Daley said." The protest, signed by Singer, the Reverend Jesse Jackson, Patty Crowley, and seven others, was filed on March 30.

Innumerable meetings followed, many of them in lawyers' offices. Agents of Daley went to court on April 19, seeking an injunction to block the challengers' efforts. Attorneys for Singer filed a countersuit. On the evening of Thursday, June 22, Daley went a step farther. The challengers were holding caucuses in eight locations that night to elect formally their challenging slate. Hundreds of Daley's jeering, foot-stomping backers appeared at seven of the meetings, demanded that they be opened to the public, and forced adjournment. Patty had been accompanied by Pat to her district's meeting at a YMCA. "I was really frightened that day! There was a crowd there, police and everything. It was supposed to be an open, free meeting and it was so . . . put on. It got very bitter. We had these four kids with us and we were afraid they were going to get hurt. Pat got us out of there, but it did open our eyes to the pressures of politics and power and how Daley can be. He just tried to wreck this thing."

Singer's people dispersed and reconvened in private, picking 51 of 59 challengers. Two days later they met again. Jesse Jackson, claiming to have received threats against his life Thursday night, appeared with bodyguards. The mayor's son led another raid of hundreds, seizing the microphone from the meetings' chairman. Twenty minutes later, as scuffles broke out, he led his men out. Singer's people then elected the final eight delegates.

Ironically, Patty, one of the original ten protesters, was not among the 59 chosen. It was not until later that she, Cathy, and Al were named alternates on the challenging slate. "The whole thing was a joke in a way, and then it got more and more serious. They raised money for all of us to go down to Florida. We went—Pat went with us—and it began to get worse and worse down there."

On June 30, after the Democratic Credentials Committee made its decision on the California delegation, it sustained the Singer challenge in Illinois. Both rulings were promptly taken to court. In no time they reached the United States Supreme Court, who ruled on July 7 that no court could intervene in an internal dispute of the Democratic party and that the business of seating delegates was up to the convention. But a day later Judge Daniel A. Covelli of the Illinois Circuit Court ruled that Singer's delegates had not been elected by the people or through the laws of the state of Illinois and issued an injunction forbidding them to take seats at the convention. If anyone did, threatened Covelli, they would be held in contempt of court and put in jail.

The conflicting decisions put Singer's delegates in a quandary. In Miami, Singer told them to decide for themselves if they would accept credentials and enter the convention. Each was called in by an attorney and asked to sign a form indicating that he or she understood the legal implications of what would take place. Pat advised Patty, Cathy, and Al against signing and suggested they drop from the delegation. Cathy and Al refused. Patty, not wanting to be the only coward, soon sided with them. All three signed and all three walked onto the convention floor when it opened on Monday evening, June 10. The next day Judge Covelli was quoted as saying the action of Singer's delegates was in "flagrant defiance" of his court order.

The convention climaxed that same Monday night when the Credentials Committee's decisions were brought to the floor. McGovern's backers played their cards deftly, bluffing when they had to, and engineered an intricate victory that regained California's 151 seats. Assured of their control of the convention, they then directed a vote to uphold the seating of Bill Singer's delegation and the ousting of Mayor Daley's. There had been talk of a McGovern compromise with Daley in which delegates from both slates would be seated with a half-vote each, but Daley refused. McGovern needed the mayor's support but could not sell out Singer so he agreed to Daley's removal. It was a move that cost him dearly in November.

Daley's delegates were seething as they stormed out. "I saw how politicians acted and it was very disillusioning," says Patty. "Pat felt embarrassed because we knew some of them and his children had kicked them off the floor."

As McCarthy backers, Patty, Cathy, and Al were under intense pressure from the rest of their delegation to convert to McGovern. Cathy now discovered that Singer and Jesse Jackson played politics the way Daley did. The Singer machine had replaced the Daley machine, and it wanted her to vote for McGovern. But on Wednesday evening she and one other McCarthyite refused. Singer could not make his delegation's tally

116

unanimous, but he still had the satisfaction of seeing Illinois put McGovern over the top during the roll call of the states.

Four months later McGovern was crushed by the incumbent, Richard Nixon. Eugene McCarthy remained quiet for several years and then announced in January, 1975, that he would again seek the presidency, this time as an independent. The previous summer he had been to the Crowley apartment to enlist Pat's assistance. Once again, Pat promised his wholehearted support.

Pat never lost faith in McCarthy. Though Patty and everyone around him disagreed, he always felt McCarthy could attract a large following, implement his ideas, and even win the presidency. His support of the senator was based, above all, on personal attraction. Pat all but idolized him. The two had an affinity for the Benedictines, McCarthy as a one-time novice, Pat as a member of the Oblates and a self-styled abbot. Pat was drawn to the impossible; the cliché about McCarthy was that he was similarly quixotic. McCarthy struck Pat as a man of integrity who was not afraid to introduce moral questions into the political arena. Ed Stephan recalls: "Pat would talk to me constantly about Gene McCarthy, his idealism, his eloquence, his scholarly background, his catholicity in the broad sense of the term. He admired his wit and urbanity. And I think Gene McCarthy was drawn to Pat greatly. I used to kid Pat, 'Gene McCarthy has as much chance of being president as I have.' He'd say, 'Don't you think that. He's going to make it.' I remember going to parties at Pat's house when Gene was there. He mesmerized everybody."

Pat's relationship with Mayor Daley, another of the protagonists in '68 and '72, was a curious mix. According to Stephan, "Pat admired Daley's skills as a mayor but thought he was old-school and not very attentive to minority problems in the city—a bricks-and-mortar guy close to the business establishment. Pat was plowing other fields. I think he and the mayor were friendly and I think the mayor called upon him from time to time to do things, which he did willingly. But ideologically they were at opposite poles."

Daley embittered Cathy and Patty but not Pat, even though he knew firsthand of the mayor's strong-arm tactics. "The mayor liked Pat," says Patty, "even though he knew some of the things he stood for, knew he was for McCarthy. Pat was never afraid of talking to Daley. He never got anything at all out of Daley, but Daley would recognize him."

Daley recognized Patty, too. Even though the Supreme Court had ruled that the seating of the Illinois challengers was up to the convention, Daley's lawyers went to court to have Singer and his delegates punished for violating Judge Covelli's order. Patty was frightened the day she appeared in court because "Daley was powerful and could do awful things if he wanted to." The case lingered for two-and-a-half years until the Supreme Court again ruled in Singer's favor, affirming that political parties had the need and the right to make rules that supersede state law. The challenge delegation had not acted illegally.

In their years of working for McCarthy, the Crowleys contributed no more than a thousand dollars to his campaigns. "We couldn't give a lot of money," Patty states, "but we could organize a party without too much trouble. I always did it by myself. Lots of times I had buffet. Pat loved to talk about how I got my food because it was a big hoax. I cheated. I bought frozen. Chicken tetrazzini, very delicious. Stouffer's. And everybody thought I slaved all day long, and I usually let them think that. They'd say, 'How do you make it?' And I'd say, 'That's a secret.' One time Ann Landers, a great fan of McCarthy, was here for dinner. We had McCarthy here. *She* has lots of money, a maid and chauffeur, etc., and she's fancy and proper—and very nice. She had her secretary call me the next day to find out what kind of vegetables I had, they were so delicious. They were frozen Japanese-style vegetables."

Over the years many causes were given a hearing in the Crowley apartment. Anywhere from fifty to a hundred and fifty would come to dinner and hear Caesar Chavez, Bernadette Devlin, Sister Elizabeth McAllister, or others less well known. The Crowleys supported numerous organizations by serving on their boards, often as chairpersons, and raising money for them. Some were the Human Rights Commission of Illinois, the Catholic Interracial Council, Catholic Scholarships for Negroes, the American Indian Center of Chicago, Business Opportunities for the Blind, the Self-Help Action Center, Marillac House of Chicago, the Catholic Labor Alliance and its later manifestation, the Catholic Council on Working Life. In the fall of 1968 the Crowleys responded to the initiatives of Rabbi Robert Marx and Father John Pawlikowski and helped develop a series of dialogues between Jewish and Catholic leaders in Chicago. The bimonthly meetings have continued for more than a decade.

Yet it was not causes but individuals who attracted Pat. If he liked an individual, he would offer a forum for his or her cause, letting friends decide if they wished to support it. One of his favorites was Renault Robinson, a black Catholic who founded Chicago's Afro-American Patrolmen's League. Pat and Patty met Robinson on a plane with Father George Clements, were instinctively drawn to him, and began to work with his organization on a variety of fund-raising ventures. Robinson was an enemy of the political establishment in Chicago and under continual harassment from the police department. Few Crowley friends found it possible to support people like him because, in Patty's words, "A lot of Catholic and Jewish people with money are involved with the city. They are getting money and business from the city and they have to be careful or they'll be crossed off. Pat was very independent. He stuck his neck out for people like Renault Robinson who were not thought of very highly in city government."

Though Pat was a broker of causes other than his own, some venture the opinion that he himself would have made an excellent politician. They cite his ability to communicate with the masses, to bring people together, and to keep his cool. Pat loved the occasions when he stumped for McCarthy, but he never entertained seriously the possibility of running for office (Patty and Marietta would have cried, "Foul"). Law partner Frank Karaba, who disagreed with Pat on McCarthy and Daley, whose Republican vote always canceled Pat's Democratic one, thinks Pat "would have made an excellent Democratic senator from the state of Illinois. He did not have the political base from which to start, of course, and he lacked the endorsement of the regular party. But if someone had been in a position to appoint Pat as a senator to fill a vacancy, it would have been an ideal appointment."

Perhaps Marietta Caron sensed more than she knew when she swore Pat to a nonpolitical life in 1937.

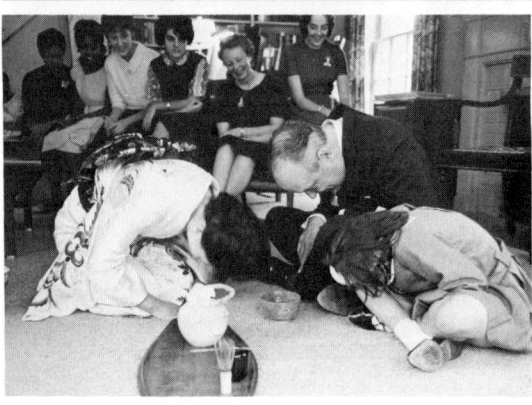

The first foreign students, 1953. Sonia Kucera of Czechoslovakia (upper right) and Petra Herms of Germany (second from left).

Pat and Theresa learn a Japanese tea ceremony.

CHAPTER ELEVEN
THEY CAME FROM MANY LANDS

Always room for one more.

Collette Fernandes, the last foreign student, and husband Ryan Gugeler.

Students from India, Haiti, Cuba, Ethiopia, Japan, and Panama in front of 2304 Elmwood.

Sister Mary Patrick, O.S.B., enjoys a Father's Day rendition of "This is Your Life."

The children marry: Mary Ann (1971), Patrick (1965), Cathy (1978).

Sonia Kucera was the first. "I was born in Czechoslovakia in 1927. I was an only child and lost my parents in early childhood. At first I lived with relatives and later, at about age nine, I came to live with close friends of my parents. I stayed with them through my adolescence.

"I was always interested in medicine but I grew up during the Second World War when things were very difficult. Since the study of medicine appeared unrealistic, particularly for a girl, I decided to become a midwife. In the meantime, since I was too young to enter the school for midwives, I entered a school specializing in children's care. A short time before I was to graduate, I was asked by my advisor if I would be interested in becoming a governess for a diplomatic family that was going to Denmark. Although I never thought about being a governess, I wished to see Denmark, and the position appeared acceptable to me.

"As fate would have it, my future employer was reassigned, and instead of going to Denmark, he was appointed chargé d'affaires to the Holy See, and we all went to Rome. I lived in Rome for almost three years. Then, because of the coup d'état in Czechoslovakia, my employer resigned from the diplomatic service and in time emigrated to the U.S.A. with his family. I came with them. That was in the fall of 1948.

"By this time I was thinking of returning to school, but though I knew some French and Italian, I did not know any English. Through the help of friends of the people I came in with, I was invited by Benedictine sisters in Lisle, Illinois, to work in their school and to learn English. I was one of three foreign students who were with them at the time. Another was Belgian and the third Chinese. In return for the opportunity to stay at the school, we were assigned minor household duties.

"At that time the sisters employed a lay teacher of English who was partly disabled and in a wheelchair. It was one of my duties to take this lady downstairs after classes and to wait with her until her taxi picked her up. This gave us an opportunity to get better acquainted.

"After a while this teacher became anxious for me to see how American families lived. Also, she felt that I would profit in my spoken language by that encounter. She spoke about me to her sister who lived in Wilmette and who belonged to the same CFM group as the Crowleys. Somehow the question of foreign students had come up during one of their CFM meetings. The Crowleys were interested in me, contacted me, and invited me to spend Christmas with them. It was 1949, and, as the family saying goes, I came for Christmas and stayed four years.

"After Christmas I was invited to come for Easter. Before the school year was over, the Crowleys said I would be welcome to stay with them during the summer until I decided what I wanted to do. So I came. That summer seems to mark my real entry into the United States. I joined the family, I guess you can say, forever.

"During the summer I realized that the best way for me would be to go back to school. The Crowleys offered to let me stay with them and helped me find a job which provided some money for tuition. They also helped me enroll at Mundelein College. The next four years, 1950 to 1954, I stayed with the Crowleys, worked part-time, and finished college.

"Before graduation from college I decided I would like to continue studying bacteriology. I thought I would first work for a couple years to save some money, but the Crowleys suggested that it would be better if I continued my studies right away since I was a few years older than the average student. They offered to lend me some money for that purpose. I took their offer, enrolled at the University of Illinois in Champaign-Urbana, and was fortunate enough to secure an assistantship in the second semester and thus become financially self-supporting.

"After I received a Master's Degree in Science in 1956, I was offered a research position at the University of Chicago. It was then that I met my husband Joseph, who was a graduate student in history at the university. He is also of Czech origin and emigrated to the United States in 1954. My real exodus from the Crowleys came when they married me off to Joseph in 1958. We were wed in Wilmette with Dad leading me up the aisle and the reception at home, 2304 Elmwood.

"1961 was our big year since our son Mark arrived on January 15. He was quite a long-expected baby, for we waited two-and-a-half years before the adoption came through. He's our only child and, of course, Crowleys' godson. Joe finished school that summer, and in 1962 was offered a position at the University of North Carolina in Chapel Hill. We have been here since. After Mark started school I went back to my profession and I am still working in research in bacteriology."

Before Sonia's first Christmas with the Crowleys, several of Chicago's original CFM groups had made inquiries about war refugees. Algie Augustine was living with the Crowleys when Sonia arrived. Some groups had adopted German families overseas and sent steady supplies of food and clothing. When a German priest visited the Crowleys in 1950 and told them of the difficulties of East German refugees, they responded by housing the Heinz Kuhn family until they settled into a home in Milwaukee.

Along with aiding refugees, CFM couples looked into the dilemma of foreign students. "In one of our early inquiries we tried to find out how many foreign students there were in Chicago, and we found out there were a lot," Patty recollects. "We decided as an action for one meeting to invite two foreign students to Thanksgiving dinner. We didn't know any so we went out to try to find two. We called the Chancery and asked if they knew any. They didn't. (Of course, there were only about ten thousand in Chicago!) They told us to call the YMCA, who had a program for foreign students. So we got two Philippine students, who to this day are great friends of ours. These were two Catholic students who'd been here at Northwestern for three years, and we were the first Catholic family they'd ever met. And you know how Catholic the Philippines are! That awakened us a lot. It made us realize that one of the things we could do was welcome foreign students into our home."

The Crowleys then enrolled in the Exchange Student Program of the National Catholic Welfare Conference. Established initially to improve relations with Germany after the war, the program brought to the United States Catholic high school students from Germany and Austria, and later, from all over the world. Petra Herms, a bright, dynamic girl who came from Germany in the summer of 1953, was the first to spend a year with the Crowleys. She was followed by Maria Pinto, a temperamental Bolivian, who proceeded to fall down the stairs and break a leg. Then came Michele Gouard, whose introduction to America was no less rude. Her trunk was burglarized on the boat from France and her pocketbook stolen on the train from Washington. When she finally arrived at the station in Chicago, she saw a huge sign on the platform—"Welcome to Chicago, Michele." Beneath it were the Crowleys. Two days later at dinner "Daddy" asked her, "Do you think you can stand it here?" Confused by his Yankee English, Michele stood up.

A warm, sensitive person, Michele recalls marvelous conversations with "Daddy" as he drove her to school each morning. She had been asked by a cab driver in Washington what she thought of Negroes, so Pat discussed race relations in the United States. When she asked him why she had not yet met a gangster in Chicago, he responded, "Gangsters are no longer those who carry a gun in the streets."

By the time Michele returned to France, the number of foreigners living with the Crowleys had multiplied. All manner of routes brought them for a week, a month, a summer, a year or more. Jean Bourland from France, Liana Stigliani from Italy, Dinh Tran and Stella Tan from Vietnam, the Takagi family and Michiko Sakamoto from Japan, Pina Fernandez from the Philippines, the Armattos from Ghana, three LaraPena children from Venezuela, Georgia and Anna Lau from Hong Kong, Penama Tharayil from India, Pat Burns from New Zealand, Peggy Clark from Australia, Elena Beck from Cuba, Claudette Austin from Trinidad, Judith Reyes from Columbia, Joseph Vandargen from the Malay States, Alicia Wong and Gloria Gamboa from Panama, the

Englanders from Chile, Juan Latapi from Mexico, Tseghe Marian and Mulu Christos from Ethiopia, Mary Claude Noel and the Paul sisters from Haiti, Francisco Callejos from Nicaragua, Livia Bueno from Brazil, Washington Odongo from Kenya, Norma Strada from Argentina, the Lamses from Detroit, Michigan. The names reach into the hundreds and the countries approximate forty.

Only a few came through the Exchange Student Program. Some learned of the Crowleys through visitors who had spent an evening at their home. Others came with a friend to spend a holiday season. A few needed a home before and after surgery or the birth of a baby, and one was sent from Tasmania by her future husband for two months of "training." One Christmas President Kennedy flew a planeload of Kenyans to the States and three of them—"big African men," says Patty—spent the holidays in Pat and Patty's bedroom. The Crowleys had huge international parties on Thanksgiving, Christmas, New Year's, and Easter. Fifty from five continents, including Moslems and Hindus, came to Christmas dinner in 1959. Seventy-five celebrated the New Year a week later, and twenty countries were represented at a party the following Easter. The numbers never diminished. If a person with an accent hailed a cab in Wilmette, the driver automatically took him or her to 2304 Elmwood.

Patty remembers one interesting arrival in the winter of 1963. "Some priest from Africa had asked us to take this girl for just a little bit. She was supposed to come to live with her husband who was in Oklahoma. Well, she arrives from Nigeria and gets off the plane. I'll never forget it! It was in the middle of winter, snow all over, and she had nothing but a light dress on. She had come from hot Africa, right from a village in Africa. The first thing she does in the car is tell us that her husband is divorcing her. We had a fit because we thought she'd only stay a short time and go live with him. She didn't know anything about how to dress or how to live. She was very heavy. One of the students sat down with her and told her she had to lose weight and bathe herself. We had to buy her clothes because she had no winter clothes. Then we went to Mundelein College and discovered that she or the nuns in Africa had lied. She hadn't even graduated from high school.

"But they did take her at Mundelein and she did very well in the long run—very well. We tried to get her marriage annulled because the nuns had made her marry this guy, but the Church wouldn't do anything about it. But finally, when she went back to Nigeria, she married someone else anyway. She's very happily married."

Nearly all the foreigners who stayed any length of time were women, and many felt especially close to "Dad." "Dad always told me he was expecting great things from me," says Monique Paul, a Haitian who later became an economist. "He'd tease me and tell me I'd be the next Barbara Ward. At dinner he would say grace and ask each of us, 'What have you learned today?' He would compliment Mom about her cooking, or he would compliment us about something or other. Then he would add, tongue-in-cheek, 'Of course, my standards are very low.' " Not wanting to lose touch with his "daughters," Dad began mimeographing a family newsletter in 1958 and asked to hear from them. Every few months a record of graduations, new jobs, weddings, births, and deaths reached his growing family throughout the world.

In addition to students came numerous overnight guests—priests, prelates, and lay people—some of whom returned to their countries to initiate CFM groups. Julius Nyerere, future president of Tanzania, spent a night in 1956, and his countryman Cardinal Lucian Rugambwa dined on several occasions. From Uganda came Benedicto Kiwanuka, who later rose to prominence in his country and then disappeared when Idi Amin came to power. Genevieve Caulfield, a blind woman from Virginia, spoke of her efforts to begin schools for the blind in Japan, Thailand, and Vietnam. A Russian couple who had studied Mark Twain at UCLA spent four days while Nikita Krushchev banged his shoe on the table at the United Nations. Patsy recalls how her father led the dinnertime conversations: "By the end of the meal my father would have someone I thought a bore talking about something that was just fascinating. I don't know how he did it. There'd be a little chuckle or some humor and all of a sudden so much would come out of a person." After dinner everyone adjourned to the living room and sat in a circle on the floor to hear the guests say something about their homelands and sing a song or recite a verse in their native language.

Everyone was welcome. Monique was still with the Crowleys when a man called one afternoon and asked to talk to Patty. "So Mom, as usual, said, 'Okay, come on over for dinner.' As far as we were concerned, this was nothing new. Every night at the last minute five or six people would show up and we would squeeze in at the table. So the man came and had a very pleasant dinner. After he had talked for a while, Dad drew a few of us aside and said, 'You know that man is really a salesman. He's selling encyclopedias!' "

In 1959 a newcomer to Chicago captured the hearts of the Crowleys and engaged them for a lifetime. Armand Marquiset was a French nobleman who in 1945 founded the Little Brothers of the Poor, a lay order whose philosophy was "flowers before bread." The poor, Marquiset believed, deserved beautiful things, not just the necessities, so his brothers brought flowers, wine, and exquisitely prepared meals to their homes. Marquiset established five houses in France, one in Morocco, and one in Italy before coming to the United States to start a mission for old people in Chicago. Pat did legal work for the Little Brothers, became their secretary, and spent many Saturday mornings with his son Patrick bringing dinners to elderly persons confined to their rooms.

All during this time Pat and Patty were nudging CFM to develop programs on behalf of foreigners. Articles in *Act* described the difficulties of visitors from overseas and deplored the lack of a large-scale Catholic response. In 1955 the National Coordinating Committee created an International Student Committee "to provide home hospitality for foreign visitors in the Chicago area." Expressing the hope that the foreign student program would become national in scope, *Act* in 1958 commended CFM couples who already had helped "countless students" by giving them homes and helping them find summer jobs. *For Happier Families* included inquiries on immigrants and refugees, and CFMers responded, sponsoring in 1960 several hundred Dutch-Indonesian refugees and providing the State Department in 1961 with a list of couples who could be called on for emergency hospitality. About the same time Cuban families threatened by Castro began to send their children to the United States. Patty remembers the night she invited CFM couples to her house to discuss the problem. "A priest from Catholic Charities was there and said CFM wouldn't do a thing about it. Within an hour we had sixty kids placed in homes. He never got over it. People took Cuban children for a year or more until their parents came. It wasn't easy, but the method of CFM had made them feel their responsibility."

Several corporations sprang from CFM involvement in international life. In 1955 World Imports, Inc. was established to provide a market for handmade items from villagers and small family cooperatives in developing areas of the world. Under CFMer Ned Taylor it evolved into a successful business venture. More important was the Foundation for International Cooperation, launched in 1960 "to collect and disseminate information concerning all phases of lay volunteer work and hospitality for overseas students." Early grants of the foundation were made to determine the status of African students in the United States, to open a family-life center in a low-income section of Mexico City, and to pay the travel expenses of American lay volunteers working abroad. FIC then turned to finding summer and part-time work for foreign students. In 1963 a federal grant was obtained for an office that disbursed emergency aid to those who had found jobs. Six hundred students from twenty-five states applied that year, but only a hundred could be helped. Later projects included medical assistance "vacations" in South America for North American doctors and huge family exchanges between the United States and other countries.

Pat and Patty later were appointed to the boards of Chicago's United Nations Association and International Visitors Center. Pat became president of the former and Patty of the latter. Among their responsibilities was the reception in 1972 of a troupe of acrobats from mainland China.

Most of their dealings with foreigners centered on students, however, and Pat did not hesitate to use his connections to help those he knew personally. An Indian, Val Valsan, was given a job at the CFM headquarters, and Monique Paul obtained summer work at the Belgian consulate. Pat used acquaintances like Senators Adlai Stevenson and Charles Percy, a former next-door neighbor in Wilmette, to help students who wanted to extend their stay in this country and had problems with the Immigration and Naturalization Service. In retrospect, the Crowleys wished more students had returned to their countries where their skills would be put to use. But at the time, they and CFM believed that their hospitality was building ties with future leaders of the emerging nations.

It is a wonder that Pat and Patty's hospitality was abused no more than it was. Usually it was other students and their own children who guarded against any exploitation of "Mom and Dad." Sonia was deeply disturbed by guests who refused to help around the house, who took their food and shelter for granted, who never even sent a word of thanks. "Frankly, I think I myself got more upset than Pat and Patty about how careless some people were. In one instance where I saw a person actually taking things, I told Pat about it. He told me he knew, that he had watched the person before and realized what was going on. But, he said, considering what enrichment came to their lives through knowing all the other people, it was a small price to pay."

Pat and Patty's own children knew only the life of constant company. While Sonia came in 1950, Patsy was finishing the fifth grade at St. Joseph's in Wilmette. (Chicken pox or not, she was displaced from her bedroom.) When it came time for high school, the family settled on St. Scholastica because its location within Chicago would expose Patsy to the city's diversity. It was also run by Pat's favorite religious order, the Benedictines. But St. Scholastica refused to admit Patsy because she lived outside the school's boundaries. So Patty devised another approach: to win the subscription drive of Chicago's archdiocesan newspaper and obtain a scholarship to the school of her daughter's choice. "We worked like mad and sold I don't know how many subscriptions to the *New World*. Patsy won, so we could choose any school we wanted. I always remember the head of St. Scholastica then. She was a very severe nun. We came down and said we wanted to enroll Patsy. She said she couldn't come. I said, 'We're sorry but she won a scholarship.' Of couse, she couldn't say a word."

The Benedictines never regretted admitting Patsy, and Patsy never regretted working so hard to get in. She sparkled academically, was active in YCS, and brought foreign students to the campus. After a year at Trinity College in Washington, D.C., she informed her parents that she wanted to become a Benedictine. Sonia, who saw Patsy as a "future mother of twelve," cried all through *The Nun's Story* after the decision was announced to her. Patsy visited Petra and Michele in Europe in the summer of 1958 and entered the convent at St. Scholastica in September. Ten months later, she received her habit, taking the name Sister Mary Patrick. (Pat couldn't argue with his daughter's choice of names, even though he preferred "Catherine Frances Mary" because of its acronym.) In 1960 Sister Patrick pronounced her first vows at a ceremony attended by Archbishop Young of Tasmania, who happened to be staying at the Crowley home, and in 1965 she took her final vows. In the years between she taught French and English and directed St. Scholastica's YCS.

Pat was extremely proud of his daughter and wrote to and about her as if she were the embodiment of Benedict's spirit. His family newsletter, in fact, was begun when she entered the convent, and its early issues were filled with excerpts from her letters. Pat's involvement with St. Scholastica grew to the point of creating and chairing its first fund-raising body, the President's Council, in 1970.

Mary Ann was altogether different from her older sister. On the day Michele arrived in Chicago, she was overwhelmed by Mary Ann's fretting. "Mary Ann told me, 'Do you realize I am going to join high school? How shall I manage?' And I thought it was very easy to join high school, so I told her, 'Do you realize that I am going to be a senior in a few weeks? How shall I manage with my bad English?' She thought it was much more terrible for her anyway."

Mary Ann was right. Sacred Heart, chosen to avoid Patsy's shadow at St. Scholastica, *was* terrible. In her sophomore year she transferred to Regina Dominican, a new high school opened in Wilmette as an outgrowth of a CFM inquiry. Though she struggled academically, Mary Ann felt at home at Regina and graduated in 1961. Then she enrolled in Immaculata College in Washington, D.C., but got homesick and switched after a year to DePaul in Chicago. Graduating in 1966 after a successful senior year, she joined the Extension Volunteers for a year of teaching at a poor parish in Kiln, Mississippi.

For years Mary Ann had resented the presence of so many people in her home, but in Mississippi her feeling began to change. She wrote long letters to her parents thanking them for their patience with her during difficult times. "My hope boils down to this," she said, "that I may follow you in all the good example you have given me. So many times I have four children. On holidays Mary Ann makes a point of inviting to her home people to strive for the motto of your mother, Dad, to live every day as it comes and do the best work possible."

When Mary Ann returned South in 1969 to teach in New Orleans, she met Gary Kono, a Japanese Hawaiian who was a manufacturing engineer for General Electric The two were married on July 31, 1971, in Chicago's Holy Name Cathedral and now have four children. On holidays Mary Ann makes a point of inviting to her home people with no place else to go, and she keeps in close touch with Mary Ann Keenan Vann, one of the foster children who seemed like intruders so many years before.

Patrick was in his teens when the Crowleys' "extended" family was at its largest, and he kept his distance from everybody. Loud, rebellious, a poor student, he was, in Michele's words, "a very, very good kid who wanted to pretend he was not. He would have been furious if somebody had told him he was a good kid." Patrick bounced in high school from Loyola to St. Procopius to St. Gregory to New Trier. He wore a black leather jacket and started drag-racing as soon as he had a driver's license. One day he invited his father to the Union Grove Dragway in Wisconsin where his '56 Ford was pitted against some of the sport's best. While his son's car stood : line to race, Pat climbed in to see if he could make as much noise as the other drivers. Not knowing Patrick's car had a muffler and the others did not, Pat floored the accelerator and blew the engine. The car was towed seventy-five miles back to Chicago.

While at St. Gregory's, Patrick met Carol Thomes, a girl from a large German Catholic family. The two were married immediately after high school on September 4, 1965, six years before Mary Ann's wedding. Patrick tried a year of college at St. Thomas in Minnesota and then went to work for Caron International. After Patrick III was born in 1966 and Philip in 1969, the family moved to Baltimore, Maryland, where Patrick became manager of an O'Brien paint store and Carol bore the twins Bethany and Tamara. Patrick's wife, children, and business have had a settling effect on him. "I think Pat would have loved to have him be a lawyer," his mother says, "but I think that we learned more and more how important it is to accept people as they are."

Cathy, the last of the Crowleys' biological children, was not yet three when Sonia celebrated that first Christmas at 2304 Elmwood. Self-reliant, sensitive, wanting to please, she thrived in the presence of so many people. It was she who helped Michele with her English. "It's easy to practice with children because they very seriously tell you that you have made a mistake," Michele says. "Adults are too polite, so they don't tell you, and you make no progress at all. Cathy was a bright girl and I talked with her a lot. She was happy to live, happy to be on earth, and always enthusiastic—full of peps, I think you say. Before a party she'd get one of those beautiful little dresses on and then wouldn't move at all because she knew she was being so pretty."

Even though her sister was on the faculty at St. Scholastica, Cathy attended that school and became a YCS enthusiast. In her senior year she was joined by Naomi Sogie-Thomas from Sierra Leone and Norma Franchi from Argentina, and after graduation the three of them toured California. A love of Cathy's was the piano, and she chose Webster College near St. Louis to further her musical education. Her father became a trustee of the school and had its president, Sister Jacqueline Grennan, speak at a CFM convention. Cathy spent the summer of her junior year working for Gene McCarthy and after graduation in 1969 went to Paris for further study. But her dreams of become a concert pianist went the way of the McCarthy campaign, and the early 1970s found her dispirited and disillusioned. On a Caribbean cruise in 1978, however, she met Trinidadian Clyde George, a leader of a calypso band. The two were married in a small ceremony on July 4 and provided their own entertainment at the reception, Clyde's bells and steel drums blending with Cathy's piano.

Theresa, the foster child who never left, was finally adopted by Pat and Patty when she was ten. For many years she was the only child in the house, and everyone doted on her. At parties Cathy would play the piano and Theresa would climb on a chair and lead the singing. *Look* magazine once prepared an article on her but space was preempted by the assassination of John F. Kennedy. In the words of Monique, Theresa was "a typical spoiled American child. Mom and Dad gave her everything and all our visitors just adored her. She was a very smart little kid, somewhat fresh, I must confess."

Theresa—"T.C." to her friends—concurs. "A lot of times I really wished we had a nice little dining-room table, just the family there, everything nice and cozy. So I'd pull things like, 'Nobody loves me, nobody loves me.' We'd have problems with the TV. Other people would be watching and I'd just change the channel. I wouldn't ask. No one ever debated what I did until Naomi came from Sierra Leone. She would turn it back to the station she was watching. She got me to say please and thank you."

T.C. was a sixth-grader when her parents made the difficult decision of leaving Wilmette for a home closer to work in downtown Chicago. Since five foreign students were living with them at the time, finding an apartment was no easy matter. One building turned them down because some of those students were black. When the Crowleys found another place at 1300 Lake Shore Drive, the manager balked. Asked if it was because of the black students, he said, "Well, they're young and may have wild parties."

The Crowleys applied enough pressure to get the apartment and immediately dispelled any fears by throwing a party—not a block party, since that would have been impossible, but an elevator-shaft party. "We told everyone in our elevator shaft to come and meet our family," Patty recalls. "Well, they were so thrilled with those students! By the time we left that apartment building two years afterward, all those students weren't just our students, they were their students." By 1969 the Crowleys' family had diminished, so they moved to a smaller apartment on the eighty-eighth floor of the John Hancock Building, where they had a majestic view of the city and the lake.

It was in the Hancock Building that the last of the foreign students joined their family. Collette Fernandes was a wisp of a girl from India, studying at the Art Institute in Chicago. She spent nearly six years with the Crowleys and was sometimes the only child at home.

"My ancestors came from southern India, from Goa. Goa was once a Portuguese colony, and that was how we got the name Fernandes. People took Portuguese names because it was easier to move around that way. My grandfather and grandmother came to Bombay, and since then we've been in Bombay. We've always lived in the city.

"My father labored for the Indian Railway. He worked in the administrative section. If there was an accident, he had to look into it, see what the cause was, and make a report. My mother was an artist, and she started to go to art school and work on a degree, but then she got married and became a schoolteacher. I was always at home with my grandmother, and she always painted. She used to paint saris. I watched her and pretended to paint like her. I always wanted to be an artist.

"My parents, like all Goans, were Catholic, very Catholic. My mother taught first grade at St. Anthony's Convent School, where we all went—my older sister and brother and I. Every grade had four different classes because they couldn't hold all the students. Even Hindu parents wanted their kids to go to the Catholic school because kids there were taught how to move around in societies other than their own. We had a lot of foreign nuns, German and Irish. The school started co-ed, but when I was in sixth grade, it became just a girls' school because the Irish Redemptorist fathers moved in and got all the boys.

"I went through grammar school and high school on scholarships. After I finished high school, I entered art school—the Sir Jamshed Jee Jhejebhoy School of Arts. We used to call it JJ School of Arts. Sir Jamshed was a wealthy Parsi who started the school when the British were in India. It's supposedly the best art school in Asia. It was so hard to get in, I jumped for joy when I found I could go! They didn't offer scholarships so my family had to pay for it. My parents weren't rich, but my mother . . . when it comes to education, she always found the money.

"I studied commercial art there. I stood fifth in the country in my final examination and was offered a fellowship, but I didn't take it because the school didn't offer anything more than what I had done. After I graduated, I worked for the London Press Exchange in Bombay. I'll never forget my salary: 100 rupees a month. I'd sharpen pencils and do all the dirty work, but I learned a lot. Basically I would do pasteups. The visualizer designs the ad, then he gives it to you, and you get all the components together and paste it on a piece of paper.

"In the meantime I applied to thirty art schools in the United States for a scholarship. I thought the States was the best place for advertising and textile design. Each school sent me information and catalogues, but only the Art Institute in Chicago seemed suitable for me. And then they gave me a scholarship. Oh, those were the best days—getting all the good news!

"My parents were worried about where I would stay in Chicago. There were immigration problems. I had to have so much money and someone to sponsor me. My father and my uncle and a whole bunch of people put all their bank accounts together and they managed to get the money. My sister had a friend living in Chicago, so she wrote her and asked if she knew of any hostels or any place I could live. This girl wrote back and gave Patty Crowley's name and the address of the CFM headquarters on Jackson Boulevard. She said Mrs. Crowley was well known for helping foreign students. Somehow any foreigner who comes to Chicago knows the Crowleys.

"Then my dad wrote the Crowleys, but they didn't have room for more students. They sent my dad's letter to the Wilsons, Craig and Kay. She used to work in the FIC office and had helped students. They wrote back and said they'd be glad to have me.

"I never left home before. Oh, God, I didn't know what I was going to come into! I was so afraid then. I went all by myself. When I think of it now, I can't imagine I did it, because people were telling me these horrible things about America. 'Be careful.' I don't know how I did it.

"The Wilsons met me at the airport. They were really nice people. They had three girls and a boy. One was in grammar school; one was in high school; I think the boy was in college; and the oldest daughter was in Vietnam as a nurse. I used the oldest daughter's room.

"Six months after I arrived they told me that Liz was coming home from Vietnam and that I'd have to find another place through the Art Institute. So I got into the worst experience of my life. I was hired by this family—it was horrible—I would go full-time to school during the day, and at night I would babysit for them and do dishes, and do odd jobs on the weekend, and get free board and lodging. The woman was very young, about thirty-two or thirty-three, and she used to bug me all the time. I think they were having marital problems. Never in my life did I see anybody fight like that! It used to hurt me to see how their kids—little kids—would suffer. I couldn't study. I couldn't do anything.

"While I was living with the Wilsons, Mrs. Crowley used to invite me to foreign student parties. One thing about Mrs. Crowley—she'd meet you once and she'd remember you. She'd know you by name. I used to go to church at Holy Name Cathedral, 12 o'clock mass every Sunday. Somehow every Sunday she would ask me, 'How are you doing with this family? Are you happy?' All the time she would ask me and she hardly knew me. I used to be really open with her. 'I don't think I'm happy. I just don't like it.'

"There was an Indian student living with the Crowleys, Renita D'Silva. One fine day Mrs. Crowley told me, 'Renita's going back to India. You can move in with us.' I'd been away from the Wilsons three months. It felt like forever.

"I came to the Crowleys' and—I don't know how to explain it—I didn't even feel I was in a strange place. Theresa was home and Cathy had her own place in the Hancock Building, two floors below us. The first thing Mrs. Crowley told me was 'Theresa's not very easy to get along with.' I felt Theresa just didn't want to be treated like a kid. So I treated her like somebody my age and really enjoyed myself with her.

"I remember how Theresa would hate to get up to go to school. Mom would come in and say, 'Theresa, wake up.' Theresa would never wake up. Then Dad would come storming in, 'THERESA, WAKE UP!' She was up like that. Every morning. It was really funny. He wasn't mad. He just had a way.

"Whatever the Crowleys did for their kids they did for me. There was no difference at all. If they took them to an expensive show, they got a ticket for me, too. They'd give me real expensive presents at Christmastime, just like their kids. Mom would worry when I went out with guys. Oh, she'd really get worried! She used to leave her bedroom door open until I came home at night.

"And how she could entertain! I tell you, a hundred was not a crowd for her. She used to do it so easily. If something went wrong with dinner, most people would give you a hundred and one excuses, but she was so. . . . She just burned it. Eat it or go. I met people I would never have met otherwise—Russians, Chinese from mainland China. I learned I could move around with anybody and not feel like something different.

"Dad was fantastic. What a guy! You could have so much confidence in him. After I finished at the Art Institute, I was worried about a job, and Dad said, 'Oh, don't worry, we'll do something about it.' He was going to get me into Caron, but unfortunately they used free-lance artists. So I got a job with an advertising agency in Chicago and worked on my own at night.

"Mom used to call me her artist in residence. I did art work for CFM and the Visitors' Center. The Visitors' Center was trying to get money for foreign students so Mom got me to paint this huge scroll for Mayor Daley. When I needed money to go back to India, Dad's office bought a tapestry I was working on. Then, when I wanted to go home to get married, we had a ceramics show in my bedroom. Ryan, my fiancé, and I made about two hundred pots. Mom called all her friends, and they came and bought pots from us. We both made our fares to go home to India.

"I hate to say this, but Mom and Dad mean more to me than my own parents. I am so much more mature than when I was at home. And I can talk to Cathy and Theresa and be understood. There's a cultural difference with my own brother and sister. When I go home, I fight with my parents all the time. I can't be open with them, so I never tell them anything. But my parents think the Crowleys are like gods. To my entire family nobody can touch the Crowleys.

"The way I was taught religion in India, everything was rules and regulations. If I didn't go to church on Sunday, my parents would kill me. I mean I probably would not come home that day. The Crowleys were good Catholics, but they were open to new ideas. My entire life changed under their roof. I feel now that I can do what I want to do and still feel good inside. I couldn't before. It's then that I got daring, that I put my foot down and said, 'I don't care.' Why suppress yourself when there's no reason for it?

"The Crowleys were religious people but they were not crazy religious. They were rich people but they never showed it. They never preached. They never talked to me about religion. It just happened. Whatever they said, they lived, which not many people do. You see them live and you want to live like them spiritually. People would come from all over the world and stay with them. The Crowleys didn't even know who they were, they didn't know their backgrounds, but they could open any cupboard in the house. Everyone that came to their home was always happy."

CHAPTER TWELVE
THE SUMMER AND WINTER OF CFM

At the third convention of MFC, Rio de Janeiro, 1963. With Pat and Patty in the top picture are Tom and Dorothy McBryan of Detroit, and Cathy.

General Session at Notre Dame's Stepan Center, scene of the 1965 CFM convention.

In 1960 the fresh air sweeping into the Catholic Church through John XXIII's open window warmed and invigorated the Christian Family Movement, but by 1970 a freezing wind was threatening to leave it cold and desolate.

The first half of the decade was glorious. CFM felt John's Vatican Council ratify its very soul, blessing the spirit—"you are the Church"—that quickened it in 1943. Documents on the Sacred Liturgy, the Church, the Apostolate of the Laity, and the Church in the Modern World spoke a language *Act* and the inquiry booklets had been using for fifteen years. And while the council helped CFM, it is also true that CFM helped the Council by preparing tens of thousands of adult Catholics for its eventual proclamations.

In the few years of his papacy John not only convoked a council but also issued two remarkable letters, *Mater et Magistra* and *Pacem in Terris*, that stimulated inquiry themes, convention talks, and *Act* editorials, becoming the core of CFM's official response to social upheaval in the United States. *Mater et Magistra* was a social encyclical in the tradition of Leo XIII's *Rerum Novarum* and Pius XI's *Quadragesimo Anno* that made explicit reference to the Cardijn technique of Observe-Judge-Act. In the September 1961 issue of *Act*, editor Donald Thorman called the document "a kind of Magna Charta for CFM" and a "vindication" of the previous year's controversial program on international life. A year later popular moralist J.D. Conway wrote in the same pages:

> If you hold that economic acitivities should be free of moral restraints and should be regulated only by free competition, that the only sound economic motive is personal profit; that the State should refrain from all intervention in the business world, then you have been out of step with official Catholic teaching for 70 years.
>
> Have you been opposed to foreign student exchange? To the rights of immigrants? The principles of the Peace Corps? . . . To idealistic concepts of a world community? Then you need to read *Mater el Magistra* carefully, as a humble Catholic, with deep faith in the Church as Mother and Teacher.[1]

Pacem in Terris, issued by Pope John on April 11, 1963, held special meaning for Pat Crowley. Invited to Rome to participate in a small paraconciliar deliberation, Pat had an inspirational audience with John several weeks after the encyclical and only five weeks before John died. Pat also deepened a friendship with Monsignor Pietro Pavan, a principal architect of both *Mater et Magistra* and *Pacem in Terris*, and persuaded him to address the CFM convention that August. A year before, Pat had become a director of the Fund for the Republic, which supported the Center for the Study of Democratic Institutions in Santa Barbara, California. After John's encyclical the Fund decided to sponsor an international symposium entitled *Pacem in Terris* and involved Pat in the preparations. Held in New York in February of 1965, the conference was successful enough that regional meetings were held over the next two years to discuss its report. In 1967 a second international symposium was convened in Geneva, and over the years two more followed. All were promoted in the official channels of CFM.

Pope John's *Pacem in Terris* discussed not only world peace and justice but also "universal and inviolable" rights of man that "cannot in any way be surrendered." A number of CFM couples applied John's statement to the question of black civil rights in the United States. The Crowleys were delighted to see some of them at a January, 1963, meeting of the Conference on Religion and Race, an organization whose steering committee Pat later joined. In June, 1963, Patty was invited to a meeting of religious leaders at the White House and heard President Kennedy reiterate principles of his June 11 television address on civil rights. *Act* subsequently published excerpts from that speech alongside compatible statements from John's *Pacem in Terris*.

At the CFM convention that August, Mathew Ahmann, executive secretary of the National Catholic Conference for Interracial Justice, asserted that laity often failed to support their bishops' statements on race relations. CFMers needed "significant interracial experiences" to get themselves moving. Accordingly, in 1964, *Act* got behind Friendship House's national program of home visits between black and white couples and supported passage of the Civil Rights Bill. The 1964-65 inquiry, "Politics and Race," suggested a number of civil rights projects for action groups, and *Act* reported on CFMers who had demonstrated in Selma or Montgomery or worked on voter registration in Mississippi, commending the priests and nuns who marched with all the others. The Crowleys cherished letters telling of CFM participation in civil rights activity.

Many in CFM were irritated, however, by the 1964-65 program, just as they had been by the 1956-57 program on respecting minorities. It was easy for suburbanites like the Crowleys to talk, they said; they didn't live in neighborhoods where property values were threatened by black immigration. Pastors unwilling to support recommendations for black-white home visits pulled chaplains out of CFM and their groups floundered. Letter writers objected to *Act's* support of the Civil Rights Bill and said the list of recommended readings on race included books by avowed communists.

But others found CFM insufficiently radical and criticized it for a lack of action. Father Andrew Greeley wrote a devastating column in 1965 that relayed the harsh judgment of young people with whom he was working. Despite all of CFM's talk about the race question, they said, it neglected the inner city. "All they do is sit out in their comfortable suburban homes and *talk* about poverty," said one girl. "If they feel zealous, they may even teach their children that there is such a thing as poverty. But they never do anything about it; CFM is just talk."[2]

The sparks continued to fly as a result of the 1965-66 program on "International Life and Culture." In 1961 Birchites in the movement had objected to a similar program, and in 1964 they had opposed the Crowleys' backing of the *Pacem in Terris* symposium. Now they spoke again: "These things frighten us. CFM has no business directing its members in any manner. . . . Otherwise, CFM becomes a political pressure group and it is lost." CFM should drop the words *Christian* and *Family* "since the brand of liberal socialism you nurture strives to eradicate the family as a social unit." "I felt I should congratulate you for successfully printing the foremost leftist periodicals in the nation."[3]

One California group returned its allotment of inquiry books, protesting the edition was "much too socialistic." Pat's response, typical of thousands of letters he wrote to those who disagreed with him, was that of a teacher:

Dear Gil and Barb:

Thanks for your letter of the 18th. We are sorry that you find the program difficult. We appreciate that there are different viewpoints about the whole role of social obligations.

As far as international relations are concerned, having traveled in much of the world, we are quite conscious of the fact that there are rich nations and there are poor nations, as Barbara Ward has written in her book on this subject, and that there are millions of people who could work all day and still be unable to survive.

So we don't know that it is necessarily true that we can sit back and say work hard and everything will be fine because we've seen too much of the other and we feel that the rich nations have a responsibility to the poor nations. How this is to be carried out—by preaching to them, or by teaching them, or giving them some incentive—is really a great problem and something that Pope John addressed himself to in his two great Encyclicals and which all of his predecessor popes talked about. Sometimes people become over-zealous on one side or another but when we read what the Council is suggesting in *The Church in the Modern World,* you'll see that the areas with which CFM has concerned itself lately are the areas that we are supposed to be concerned with.

So keep up your interest and keep an open look at these problems because they are terribly complex. The Church must become involved in the world, as Pope Paul said to us in 1957 at the Lay Congress. He came here to visit at the United Nations and agreed, if he was invited, he would go to Peking if it would be of help in the peace effort. With his great example, we've got to look into it.

We hope these ideas will be of some assistance. And that you will find the programs you are looking for and will be able to develop your apostolic zeal through them, even though some of them may seem out of tune with your notions; maybe you can work them out together.

Best wishes.

Sincerely in the Holy Family,
Pat & Patty Crowley

Act at this time was reaching its peak not only in circulation—41,000 as Tim Murnane replaced Don and Barbara Thorman as editor in 1964—but also in quality. From an occasional self-congratulatory newsletter it had matured to a monthly journal of opinion that attracted authors with a national reputation. There were photographs, letters, bibliographies, book reviews, editorials, cartoons, and articles like "The Spark of Creativity," "Can We Have a Christian Art?", "World Poverty and the Christian," "Sex and the College Student," "The Disease of Starvation." Full-page color covers depicted national personalities: Goldwater and Johnson in October of 1964, the family of John Kennedy a month later. When Larry Ragan became editor in 1965, he said in his first issue: "I like a fight. By 'fight,' of course, I mean argument and debate. Nothing but good can come from healthy controversy when it deals with a subject worth considering seriously. And I don't know of any serious subjects worth considering that have only one side to them."[4]

Conventions provided another indication of growth. 1960 was the first year that the Notre Dame meeting was replaced by "area" convocations. Eleven were held that year; by 1964 the number had increased to fifteen, including one in Canada. The national event at Notre Dame, held on alternate years with area conventions, continued to swell. The 1965 meeting that introduced the controversial inquiry on international life and culture was attended by nearly 5,000, a five-fold increase in ten years. Conventioneers heard leading Protestant and Catholic liberals from the United States and around the world, among them Bernard Haring, Martin Marty, John Noonan, and Mary Perkins Ryan. The budget that year was $130,000, over a hundred thousand dollars more than a decade before. Patty had received Mundelein College's Magnificat Medal in 1963, and when she and Pat were honored with Notre Dame's Laetare Medal in 1966, CFM gained even more legitimacy. They were the first in the eighty-three-year history of the award to receive it as a couple.

Internationally, developments were proceeding apace. In March, 1966, Pat and Patty attempted to duplicate their world tour of ten years earlier. They began by speaking to standing-room-only crowds in New Zealand and Australia. Besieged by newspaper, radio, and TV reporters, they quickly discovered the interest was not in them but in the pill. Everyone was searching for clues to the eventual decision of the birth control commission. Pat parried questions with corny jokes, and one reporter characterized him as being "more evasive than Dean Rusk." In their twelve days in New Zealand and Australia, the Crowleys met five thousand people, including eighty-three-year-old Cardinal Joseph Cardijn. CFM seemed to be on solid footing "down under."

From Australia the two flew to Africa, where a few CFM groups had been started by Africans who had visited CFM homes in the United States. Pat learned of the special problems of the Christian family there. Many Africans lived in polygamous extended families that provided economic as well as social support. "When a Christian casts off from that extended family, he does so at a severe wrench not only to his psychological heritage but to his economic well-being," Pat wrote in *Act*. "Alone, he must fend for himself; no longer will anybody take care of him."[5] His education and professional skills ordinarily helped the Christian African, but the strains on him were enormous. African CFMers were using the same *For Happier Families* used in America, but there was talk of making translations and writing inquiries pertinent to the African situation.

The highlight of the Crowleys' stay in Africa was a chance to renew their acquaintance with Julius Nyerere, president of Tanzania, who had visited their home in 1956. Altogether they toured seven countries in March and April before they were called back to Chicago by the sudden death of Patty's brother-in-law.

In the fall of that same year, the Crowleys flew to Caracas, Venezuela, for the fourth meeting of MFC, the Latin-American CFM. After the initial 1957 conference in Montevideo, CFM and MFC had met together in Mexico City in 1960 and Rio de Janeiro in 1963. *Act* estimated that thirty thousand copies had joined MFC in its first decade (it did not guess how many had dropped out). At Caracas in 1966 the Mexican delegation proposed that an International Confederation of Christian Family Movements (ICCFM) be established to exchange information between the continents. The resolution passed and Mexico City's Jose and Luzma Alvarez-Icaza, who had originated the idea at Notre Dame in 1965, were elected first president couple of the confederation. The founding of ICCFM climaxed a year in which Pat and Patty had covered one hundred thousand miles and forty countries. They had slept in more than eighty different beds!

The Crowleys attempted to keep a low profile with regard to the Latin Americans to counter their fear of being dominated by the United States. Pat and Patty were thus taken aback in 1967 when a meeting of ICCFM in Madrid, in what became an annual event, elected them president couple. Unlike the United States CFM, which set policy for an entire country, ICCFM was simply a clearing house of news and ideas. To begin the exchange, Pat issued the confederation's first newsletter in December of 1967.

In the prime of life now, CFM in the United States had the confidence to subject itself to the examination of outside consultants. In the fall of 1966 the national Executive Committee commissioned three sociologists from the University of Notre Dame— William D'Antonio, William Liu, and John Maiolo—to survey its members and sketch the first broad portrait ever made of the movement. Before, CFM's pulse had been taken from letters to the national office, subscriptions to *Act,* program book orders, and reactions to national and area conventions. Now the vast majority of members who never voiced an opinion to the leadership would be included in the diagnosis.

In the fall of 1967 questionnaires were sent to approximately 2,000 CFM couples from 400 systematically selected action groups. At the time all of CFM's vital signs were healthy. The convention in August had kept alive the tradition of being the "biggest ever," and the speakers—John McKenzie, Gregory Baum, Harvey Cox, Sidney Callahan, Gordon Zahn, Carl Stokes, Senator Mark Hatfield, among others—had been provocative.

Couples numbering 1,188 from 272 groups eventually responded to the survey. On the average they were in their mid to late thirties, had been married twelve years, had four children, and had lived at their present address only five years. Ninety-six percent of the husbands, compared with only 68 percent of American Catholic males at large, had at least a high-school education; and 92 percent, compared with only 55 percent of American Catholic men, had white-collar jobs, typically as administrators, professionals, or proprietors of medium-sized businesses. Wives had some education beyond high school but generally were not employed outside the home. Although CFMers said they were politically independent, they usually voted Democratic. The overwhelming majority of them were drawn from the first large wave of American Catholics to enter the middle class.

Was CFM effective? The rank-and-file said it had improved the religious life of their families, helped them understand their spouses and rear their children, and made them more aware of civic responsibilities. CFMers joined voluntary organizations far more frequently than other Americans of their social position and became leaders in them. There was no evidence that CFMers were joiners by nature, but a good deal showing they were influenced by the Inquiry Method to become active in their communities.

Along with the good news, however, came bad: CFM lost between a quarter and a third of its membership *every year.* Early in the project the researchers had been astonished by the number of defunct groups still on membership rolls in the national office. In some cities only half of those listed still existed, and many of them consisted of three, two, or even one couple instead of the desired five. Of currently active members, 20 percent were in their first year of CFM and only 16 percent had been in the movement more than five years. The average term of membership was three and one half years. So far CFM had been able to recoup its losses and still grow, but how long could it do so? The fact that only 3 percent of CFM members were twenty-five or younger suggested that the movement might limit itself to one generation.

Yet no one knew for certain whether the data boded well or ill as they were fed back to CFM leadership and the readers of *Act* late in 1968 and throughout 1969. Decisions were made in those years that affected the course of the movement far beyond the capacity of such data to comprehend. The first decision was made by the Crowleys themselves. They had run CFM as benevolent dictators, recognized and loved by innumerable local groups, for nearly twenty years. Could the movement, seemingly so healthy, now stand on its own? The Crowleys' only choice was to find out, for ICCFM, travel, and politics were absorbing more and more of their energy. When Ray and Dorothy Maldoon of Munster, Indiana, were elected chair couple of the Executive Committee in 1967, the Crowleys eyed them as possible successors. Pat and Patty continued as secretary couple of that committee, watching all the while for the opportune moment to step down.

A second decision had been building for several years. In keeping with the Vatican Council's endorsement of ecumenism, grass-roots contacts were being made with a number of Protestant laity and clergy. Protestants had observed CFM meetings and spoken at area conventions. In 1965 Fred and Adena Stitt of Evanston, Illinois, wrote an Episcopal version of *For Happier Families* and presented a seminar at the Notre Dame conference on "CFM in the Episcopal Church." A year later they accompanied the Crowleys to Caracas and became the only non-Catholic signers of the ICCFM charter, making that confederation ecumenical from the start. In the United States, a small Episcopal CFM with its own editions of inquiry books blossomed under the Stitts' direction, and in 1967 an ecumenical program book was prepared by Episcopal,

Lutheran, and Catholic couples. Dr. Eugene Carson Blake, General Secretary of the World Council of Churches, was invited to that year's convention and, although he was unable to attend, the meeting did work on means of developing an interfaith CFM.

Finally, in 1968, CFM's executive and coordinating committees decided to open the movement officially to all Christian denominations. They absorbed the small Episcopal structure, directed the program committee to write inquiry books suitable for all Christian denominations, and resolved to update all publications ecumenically. The 1969 convention would feature two Protestant speakers, Episcopal Bishop C. Edward Crowther, banned from South Africa because of his opposition to apartheid, and Joseph Sittler, professor in the Divinity School at the University of Chicago.

A third decision, momentous only in retrospect, was to sponsor a Spanish movement known as *Encuentro Conyugal*—Marriage Encounter. Pat and Patty had first learned of the movement when they stopped in Barcelona to visit MFC groups on the way home from the 1965 meeting of the birth-control commission. Begun in 1962 as an MFC service for twenty-eight working-class couples, Marriage Encounter was built around a series of exercises in which husband and wife gain the confidence to reveal their inner selves to each other. In 1966, its founders, Father Gabriel Calvo and Mercedes and Jaime Ferrer, made a presentation at the international CFM-MFC meeting in Caracas, and from there Marriage Encounter spread to Spanish-speaking couples in North and South America. At the 1967 CFM convention, Alfonso and Mercedes Gomez, a Mexican couple who had taken part in an encounter, pleaded with the Crowleys to be put on the program. They were given a few minutes to address the convention and afterward led ten couples through the marriage encounter exercises, the first time it had been done in English.

Two months later when Pat and Patty were in Madrid, they invited to the United States a contingent of Spaniards experienced in giving encounter weekends. In August of 1968, at the height of Gene McCarthy's presidential bid, a planeload of fifty couples, twenty-nine priests, and a few guitar-playing teenagers toured the United States and ran encounters, principally for the Spanish-speaking. Though the Spanish MFC paid the group's air fare to and from the States, expenses in this country were borne by the national CFM, local CFM groups, and families who offered their homes for lodging. The few encounters presented in English at the Crowleys' insistence proved to be seminal. CFMers began to push Marriage Encounter in their areas, and in January of 1969 a handful met at Elberon, New Jersey, to constitute themselves the National Executive Board for the Marriage Encounter movement. Two encounters, a training session for prospective leaders, and another meeting of the board were scheduled for the CFM convention the following August.

These three decisions were made at a time CFM began to accumulate serious financial debts. The budget had been balanced all along because of donations from friends of the Crowleys (the principal "secret angel" contributed in the neighborhood of $10,000 annually), but costs were multiplying beyond even their generosity. In 1965 the growth of the movement had demanded the hiring of an Assistant Secretary Couple, Bob and Carol Martin, and the Crowleys' impending resignation meant that more salaried staff would have to be added. In 1965, too, despite the Crowleys' objections, a dues system had been initiated. Five dollars a year covered the cost of the inquiry book, a subscription to *Act,* and the dues themselves.

But few CFMers paid, and the crisis mounted. In fiscal year 1966-67, income of $127,000 left a deficit of $13,000, and in 1967-68 income was only $115,000. The biennial conventions, which were self-supporting, were unscathed in the crunch, but questions were asked about *Act.* For years the decision had been to keep it in front of as many faces as possible. Requested or not, paid for or not, it was sent to anyone who ever wrote to the national office. Now the bills incurred by that policy came due. Was *Act's* overgrown mailing list and its lush format worth the cost to the movement?

CFM's new policies and problems would impact simultaneously on the 1969 convention, organized by Patty with the hope that it would be her last. In addition to caucuses taking up the impending Crowley resignation, ecumenism, Marriage Encounter, and CFM finances, fifteen couples, representing thirty countries, would conduct the business of ICCFM, and special meetings—the first of their kind—would be held for the Spanish-speaking.

The last seemed especially opportune in the wake of the visit of Spain's *Encuentro Conyugal*. The national office sent letters to every bishop in the country asking for his support of this phase of the convention and including a brochure detailing the entire program. But the bishops would have none of it. John J. Ward, an auxiliary from Los Angeles, responded in part:

> In looking over the program, it would be hard to sell this to our Spanish-speaking people as a thoroughly Catholic event. I see no reference on page 8 of the program to the celebration of the Mass—the summit and source of our lives. I see no reference to the participation in the event by the Chief Shepherd of the place, and among the featured speakers are two non-Catholic Bishops, C. Edward Crowther and Dr. Joseph Sittler.

It would be most difficult to sell this proposal to the Spanish-speaking people without more internal evidence that the project was led by the Bishop of the Diocese, his priests and people.[6]

Bishop Ward was mistaken in calling Professor Sittler a bishop, but he was correct in noting the absence of South Bend's "Chief Shepherd," Bishop Leo Pursley. Pursley, an early champion of the movement, was not the only ordinary to separate himself from CFM. Though the organization had never been officially endorsed by the American hierarchy, it had enjoyed the favor of certain bishops. Now, mindful of the Crowleys' disavowal of *Humane Vitae* the summer before and disturbed by the presence of Protestants, many of those bishops quietly withdrew the support the Crowleys had cultivated for twenty years.

At the convention itself, CFM's Executive Committee met to prepare for the Crowleys' impending resignation. The committee decided to reorganize itself and become the primary decision-making body in the movement, no longer an arm of the Coordinating Committee, whose role was reduced to that of sounding board. The Maldoons' title was upgraded to national president couple, and although Pat and Patty remained executive secretary couple, it was clear they would not do so for long.

The Executive Committee also ratified changes in CFM's financial structure. *Act* already had been cut to eight pages, the price of an annual subscription raised to three dollars, and instructions sent to prune the mailing list of nonpayers. *For Happier Families,* a mainstay of the movement from the beginning, was abandoned in favor of *People Are,* an ecumenical manual that would serve as the 1969-70 inquiry and then become the new introductory booklet. Five dollar dues would be charged, independently of the cost of inquiry books, whose price was set at $2.50. In addition, a fund-raising campaign was launched to reduce CFM's stack of bills.

At the same time the executive board of Marriage Encounter decided on a move that alarmed and angered the leadership of CFM. Feeling that CFM was interested in encounters as one-time experiences only, the board passed a motion stating that CFM and ME were "separate and independent movements." The Crowleys had met with Jamie and Arline Whelan, executive couple of ME, in the spring and proposed an affiliation between ME and CFM, but that offer was now rejected. Marriage Encounter's delcaration of independence broke precedent with Spanish-speaking countries, where *Encuentro Conyugal* remained securely in the structure of MFC. American CFM leaders had hoped ME would continue as a CFM service on the order of the previous generation's Cana Conference, but at the 1969 convention they were presented with an offshoot that promised to crowd out its mother plant.

These events weighed heavily on the Crowleys, who in the fall of 1969 began sending their CFM files to the Notre Dame archives in anticipation of their formal resignation. Wanting to leave a healthy organization in the hands of their successors, they raised the money to pay off CFM's debts. In December John Maiolo of the Notre Dame research team said in a press release accompanying the final report of the CFM study that the movement was on the decline. In one of his few shows of sarcasm, Pat wrote Maiolo expressing his appreciation that "CFM was spelled correctly" in Maiolo's statement. Pat then used the pages of *Act* to write as optimistically as possible of CFM's prospects. In February he wrote that "the hesitations and the turning points that were so necessary at the August meeting had been replaced by a concentrated resolve" and that "there seems to be a slow but nevertheless steady rise in CFM memberships across the country."[7] He emphasized CFM's future among Protestants, Spanish-speaking Catholics, and inhabitants of other lands. And even though Marriage Encounter was sapping the strength of CFM, Pat hailed it as one of the extraordinary new developments in the movement.

The Crowleys' official resignation was announced in the July-August, 1970, issue of *Act*. Bob and Cathy Burggraf of New York were hired by the executive committee to replace them as secretary couple, effective September 1. The following December Pat and Patty expressed their gratitude—"gratitude for these past 25 years, gratitude to all the people that we have worked with, and now, a heartfelt thankfulness to people like the Burggrafs for taking over and steering the ship in the year ahead."[8]

Despite its brave front, CFM suffered. The yearly contribution of the "secret angel" followed Pat and Patty into ICCFM and so was lost to the national movement. A change in the fee structure—one charge of $7.50 for dues, inquiry book, and a year of *Act*—brought little financial relief. Nor did any help come from a shift in programming, which allowed action groups to choose from briefer modules the inquiry themes they wished to pursue in a given year. Campaigns in 1973 to double CFM membership and to solicit contributions from former CFMers were also unsuccessful, as was a National Finance Campaign in 1974 that included the seeking of foundation support. The 1973 convention, entitled a National Seminar on Family Life because it included the first national Marriage Encounter conference, attracted only 1,200 persons. In 1975 Marriage Encounter decided to meet on its own and CFM moved its convention to St. Mary's College in South Bend because Notre Dame was beyond its means. This was also the year that *Act*, its circulation decimated in the previous decade, ceased publication.

As CFM entered its winter, Marriage Encounter experienced a springtime. Despite constant friction between rival factions in St. Paul and New York, the movement shot up as CFM had done in the 1950s. Not only did it capture the country's new mood of introspection, it drew on leaders whose skills had been honed in CFM, and it developed structures akin to its parent's. In 1969 former CFM chaplain Charles Gallagher of New York converted the idea of action cells into "Image" groups that periodically renewed an original weekend encounter. In collaboration with CFM in 1973, the St. Paul ME produced *The Encountering Couple,* a follow-up program on the order of CFM's inquiry books. And in 1974, *Agape,* once a newsletter of the St. Paul CFM confederation, was adopted as the national journal of the St. Paul movement.

A year later, the St. Paul (or "National") Marriage Encounter tried to heal its split with CFM by making *Agape* a joint publication of the two bodies. But CFM continually complained of the lack of space in *Agape* and in October of 1976 dropped its affiliation with that journal. At the time dues-paying members numbered 3,200.

Conservatives have argued that it was the liberal stands taken by CFM's leadership in the early sixties that were responsible for its later decline. But the Notre Dame study says otherwise: most CFM couples were pleased with the work of the programming committee. Indeed, in spite of protest mail from the right, researcher John Maiolo opined that even stronger liberal positions should have been taken.

Far more important than political positions in determining the eventual fate of CFM were the loss of the Crowleys and the sudden withdrawal of supportive bishops and clergy. The hierarchy's turnabout was telling because CFM, which emerged at a time the bishops had extraordinary power, was welded to the diocesan structure. For most of its life CFM simply did not exist without the blessing of the local ordinary. The Crowleys had constantly struggled to obtain, if not the backing of individual bishops, then at least their tolerance. So effective had been Pat's informal diplomacy that priests wanting to start CFM had often asked him to intercede with their superiors.

As essential to CFM as tolerant bishops were the clergy who served as chaplains, and the Crowleys were aware of it from the beginning. The two had worked hard, and not always successfully, at attracting priests, promoting CFM even in seminaries. Priests were excellent recruiters and their approval—and, through them, that of the Church—was often sought by a laity struggling with a new sense of independence. For twenty years national chaplain Hillenbrand was as powerful in the movement as Pat and Patty themselves. But in the late sixties, just as the hierarchy turned against CFM, an identity crisis struck the priesthood. Resignations increased and vocations decreased. Priests experimented with new roles, and some of them, including CFM chaplains, decided to marry. Though hierarchy, clergy, and the Crowleys themselves were lost to CFM for different reasons, the effect was the same. The fence on which twenty years of vines had grown was abruptly torn down.

To this removal of support was added the paradoxical effects of ecumenism. Despite the language of Vatican II, bishops viewed CFM's ecumenical thrust with alarm, for it meant a loss of control. CFM in various dioceses now included Protestants, and Catholic family-life directors had to share their power. Many decided to forget about CFM and some even reacted vengefully. In Louisiana one objected to the 1970-71 inquiry on "The Family in a Time of Revolution" by pulling three hundred couples out of the movement. When Episcopal priest Donald Jones presided over Sunday Eucharist at the 1971 convention, bishops watching from a distance and long-time chaplains like Monsignor Hillenbrand and Father Putz perceived it as the fatal climax of a series of errors. At the moment Father Jones began that liturgy, says Father Putz, "CFM lost the hierarchy and I became disinterested."

Ecumenism took its toll in other ways as well. The Catholic parish, like the Catholic diocese, was lost as a base for activities, for a group could no longer be affiliated with the worship of a particular denomination. Continuity in the spiritual life of the movement was shattered as references to papal encyclicals from *Mystici Corporis* to *Pacem in Terris* were weeded out of the new manuals. Nor was the cost of ecumenism paid by Roman Catholics alone. When the Episcopal CFM was absorbed into the Catholic structure in 1968, a large segment of the Episcopal membership refused to go along.

CFM, of course, was primarily an organization of married Catholic laity, and they, like the clergy who served as chaplains, underwent profound changes in the 1960s. The vast majority welcomed the warm breezes of Pope John and identified with the most open, progressive impulses of the Vatican Council. But John died and was succeeded by Paul VI, who raised hopes by convening a birth-control panel and then dashed them by ignoring its recommendations. *Humanae Vitae* not only estranged the American hierarchy from the Crowleys, it also alienated the American laity from the Church. American Catholics felt betrayed by Paul's ruling: is this what Pope John, the Council, the changes were all about? By 1974, 83 percent had quietly rejected *Humanae Vitae* and only a minority believed in papal infallibility. Church attendance was down and apostasy among young adults on the rise.[9] Liberals described the crisis as a plummeting of the leaders' credibility and conservatives as a shedding of the uncommitted. But both agreed that just as one encyclical ignited CFM in 1943, another came close to snuffing it out a quarter of a century later.

The climate outside the Church had also changed in those twenty-five years. A society that glorified the family in the post-war era, America came to ignore it in the 1960s. At the beginning of that decade, a wave of social activism swelled on the horizon, and in 1968 it rolled in and crashed in disillusionment on the streets of Chicago. Activists gave up, turned inward, and "encountered" each other in the sensitivity workshops of popular psychology.

The fortunes of CFM were tied to the waxing and waning of these enthusiasms. It prospered as the nation dwelt on family life and it suffered as the family fell from favor. It anticipated the activism of the sixties, then reached its peak and was spilled in the very same years. The void it left among the Catholic laity was filled by Marriage Encounter, a movement that taught couples to turn inward and communicate their deepest feelings to their partners.

"We're less, but we continue to exist, which is amazing," says Patty today. The Maldoons, who have vowed to preserve the seeds left by the movement and who, along with Patty, have resurrected *Act,* insist that neighborhoods and families—especially single-parent families—need CFM more than ever. Couples who dialogue with each other are not enough, they say. What is needed are couples who will get out of themselves and *act* on behalf of their community.

But as matters stand now, it is Marriage Encounter and not the Christian Family Movement that has captured the enthusiasm of the married Catholic laity in the United States, if for no other reason than that the 1970s are not in the 1950s. In social movements, as in lives, there are seasons—times to be born, times to die, and times to be born again.

CHAPTER THIRTEEN
ILLNESS— AND FAMILIA '74

In the Cameroons (top), with President Julius Nyerere of Tanzania (middle), and at Familia '74.

ICCFM at Kilkenny, Ireland, 1971 (top), and more scenes from Familia '74.

First *Humanae Vitae,* then the McCarthy failure, and then the malady afflicting CFM. Fate and Evil had risen menacingly in the dancer's path, but he passed them by without faltering. If Pat Crowley knew CFM was in desperate straits in the years after his resignation, he gave no inkling of it. His imagination was scanning broader horizons, and at the same time, facing the final threat.

The Christmas newsletter he wrote in 1971 sang with joy. Among details of trips, growing children, and new homes were accounts of Mary Ann's wedding in July and an historic meeting of ICCFM in October. Pictures of the bridal party and of beaming ICCFM delegates spread glad tidings to the Crowley family around the world. But one paragraph was out of tune with the rest. Pat wrote:

> The last event we'll record was Pa's operation. A very new experience suddenly scheduled May 28th. The few days before the procedure allowed time for a quick review of the wonderful life we've had to which so many of you have contributed. The doctors say the operation was a success, the chances of a recurrence slight so we're more thankful than ever and more aware of the transitory character of life and of the things that really count when one is activated to review a life and see what's of value in that quick reflection. We were reconfirmed in the attitude inherited from Grandma Crowley expressed in these few lines:
> "It is a blessed secret—living by the day. Anyone can carry his burden, however heavy, until nightfall. Anyone can do his work, however hard, for one day. God gives us nights to shut down the curtain of darkness on our little days. We cannot see beyond. Short horizons make life easier."

In the course of an ordinary physical examination doctors had discovered a lump in Pat's chest. Assuring him that the possibility of breast cancer in men was remote, they insisted on removing it immediately. Everyone expected the surgery to be routine, but the tumor was found to be malignant. A large part of Pat's left breast and underarm had to be excised.

It was a powerfully shocking experience, but once he had absorbed it, Pat preferred neither to dwell on it nor talk about it. On one occasion, after his recovery, he did tell Al Augustine he had been frightened and could not believe it was actually happening. "He said, 'Boy, that was an experience,' and then he started talking about the nurses and how well he got along with them and how they thought he was their favorite patient. He said they got to like him because he made these loud groans in a funny way. They gave him all the special services. He'd always tell about the special things people did for him in situations like that. He was so impressed by it."

If Pat was worried about a recurrence of cancer, no one in his immediate circle knew. His reaction to the doctor's report was the same as his response to *Humanae Vitae*, the 1968 Democratic Convention, and the tragic cirsis in CFM. If there were feelings of despair, he kept them to himself in an effort to protect those around him. Besides, there was no time for depression. Pat Crowley was having too much fun at this point in his life trying one impossible venture after the next.

In 1971 his work as a corporate lawyer was not dramatically different from what it had been when his father died in 1952. Formally, he was a salaried officer, second in command, in both the O'Brien Corporation and Caron International, Inc., and the senior partner in the Crowley law firm. (Technically, the latter did not become a "firm" until partners began sharing revenue in 1971.) In practice, however, he played the role in all three concerns that he did in CFM and his own family. He was the abbot of the corporations. Jerry Crowley ran O'Brien paints, John Caron presided over Caron International and Frank Karaba managed the law firm—just as Patty directed the affairs of CFM. But all were in constant, often daily communication with Pat, drawing both on his imagination and his common sense.

In the judgment of his associates, Pat Crowley was not a brilliant lawyer but a brilliant businessman who happened to be a lawyer. He was an expert in financial and tax matters. Because of his absorption in the legal affairs of CFM, FIC, ICCFM, and needy persons and causes, he did not develop his law firm to its potential. He was far more aggressive with the other family companies. Caron gradually expanded into an international corporation, and O'Brien made a series of acquisitions culminating in the purchase of California's W.P. Fuller Company in 1967—a move Jerry Crowley saw as a case of the mouse trying to swallow the elephant. Says Karaba, "Without Pat the acquisition would never have been made because on every day of our negotiations Jerry Crowley found another reason for not going ahead. Fuller was a lot for a small company to absorb. Nevertheless, Pat, who was always an optimist, felt that it would be good for the company, and he proved to be correct."

Pat's business sense was instrumental in launching his wife on another family enterprise, the travel agency, Space, Inc. In 1970, after the two had resigned as executive secretaries of CFM, Space opened its doors in an office fifty-eight floors beneath the Crowleys' new apartment in the Hancock Building. There Patty put to use her extensive traveling and organizing experience, and Cathy developed a career as a travel agent. It was, in fact, on one of her tours that she met husband Clyde George.

Despite their new business efforts the Crowleys maintained their commitment to supporting family life. Intrigued by the notion of family therapy, Pat became acquainted with the newly formed Family Institute of Chicago, was invited to sit on its board, and became its president in 1972. For years he had been attempting to freshen the air in CFM by exposing its leaders to contemporary experts on the family. Even before he and Patty stepped down as the movement's leaders, he had written to the White House, the NAACP, the Ford and Rockefeller Foundations, and the Center for the Study of Democratic Institutions to propose conferences and seminars on family life.

His first success was a small award from the Rockefeller Foundation to hold the Lake Como meeting in June, 1968. After its postponement, never being one to turn back money, Pat used his connections with Chicago's Little Brothers of the Poor to obtain the use of one of their chateaux in La Pree, France. In November of 1968, eight internationally known scholars, their spouses, several priests, and some fifteen ICCFM couples from around the world gathered to discuss family planning, conduct ICCFM business, and enjoy the cuisine of a specially hired French chef. (The food was so rich that by the end of the week participants preferred photographing it to eating it.) On the way to La Pree, Pat had conducted business for Caron International, stopped to see his daughter Michele, and invited her, her husband, and infant daughter to the conference. There she puzzled everyone by constantly referring to Pat and Patty as "Daddy" and "Mom."

The La Pree discussions were summarized in a booklet, "The Christian Family in Today's World," which contained both scholarly papers and reports from ICCFM couples on the state of the family internationally. The other outcome of the meeting was a new structure for ICCFM: a General Assembly, made up of one or more couples from each country, and an Executive Committee, comprised of one couple from each continent. The General Assembly would convene at Notre Dame in 1969 and then alternate annual meetings with the Executive Committee.

In 1970 Pat called a conference at Woodstock, Illinois, on "Family Function in the Seventies," but its recommendations to establish a Family Research and Development Center never materialized. In that same year, the six-couple Executive Committee of ICCFM met in Auckland, New Zealand; and in 1971 over fifty individuals from twenty countries gathered in Kilkenny, Ireland, to make a Marriage Encounter, sing, and adopt a five-year plan for ICCFM. A directive to exchange contacts with the World Council of Churches resulted in the addition of Leslie and Mona Clements of the Family Education Department of WCC to ICCFM's Executive Committee. The General Assembly also decided to promote family groups with non-Christians, to continue sponsorship of Marriage Encounter, and to concentrate on Africa and Asia in developing CFM internationally. Following up on the last, Pat wrote Julius Nyerere to propose an African congress on the family.

In 1972, Pat designed another conference around the meeting of ICCFM's Executive Committee in Tarrytown, New York. Margaret Mead and Thomas Cottle were among the experts who spoke to the theme of loneliness in contemporary life. Father Lou Savary, S.J., staged an impromptu meditation to music, and Father Charles Vella from Malta informed ICCFM's leaders that funds for a 1974 World Family Congress in Africa might be available from the United Nations. The United Nations, having declared 1974 "World Population Year," was anxious to support activities designed to bring about worldwide awareness of the population problem. Although Patty thought the idea of getting money from the U.N. "ridiculous," the day after the convention a committee of five was visiting an officer of the U.N.'s Population Commission. "I always thought things were impossible," she reflects, "but Pat always thought everything was possible."

It was difficult to determine the size of ICCFM in these years. International meetings, never attended by more than sixty individuals, were not the gauge of the movement's vitality that the Notre Dame conventions were in the United States. Nor was the circulation of ICCFM's newsletter in any way an indicator comparable to the circulation of *Act*. Figures such as "150,000 couples" or "200,000 constituents" from "sixty-odd countries" were bandied about in ICCFM's literature, but these were surely exaggerations. It does seem clear, however, that with the exception of England and Ireland, the international movement did not suffer the losses that the United States CFM did in the early 1970s. It is also true that most of the countries in which ICCFM existed would not tolerate the political expression exhibited by CFM in the United States.

As far as Pat was concerned, the World Family Congress targeted for Africa would be the high point of ICCFM's first decade and the peak of his own life as well. He obtained planning funds from the United Nations to permit a committee of eight to assess the feasibility of having the conference at the University of Dar es Salaam, Tanzania, in June, 1974. The Family Education Department of the World Council of Churches, headed by Les Clements, had committed itself to the project and agreed to a name: Familia '74, after the Swahili word for family. Though the United Nations had not yet agreed to support the conference itself, the signs of it doing so were propitious.

In March of 1973 the Crowleys flew to Geneva, where they picked up Father Vella, Les Clements, and WCC's Rex and Caroline Davis. The six flew overnight to Nairobi, Kenya, landing the next morning in Dar es Salaam, on the coast of the Indian Ocean.

There they met Stanford Shauri of the Tanzanian Christian Council and Chief Patrick Kunambi of the Tanzanian CFM. The following two days were spent visiting Tanzania's newest development: socialistic villages based on the African concept of Ujamaa, or familyhood. Impressed by what they saw, the eight planners decided to incorporate an encounter with Ujamaa into the assembly itself. Nyerere, who had given them permission to visit the villages in the first place, thought their idea felicitous.

Once the outline of Familia '74 was definite, Pat and Patty visited Cardinal Rugambwa, who had been to their home on several occasions. Then they flew to the Cameroons and spent several days bumping around in a Land Rover with Father Louis Nomi to see CFM groups active in the villages. In Nigeria they were entertained by their daughter Philomena Iba, who ten years before had appeared at the airport in the middle of a Chicago snowstorm looking for her husband in Oklahoma. Philomena was now married to the head of the University of Ife's Department of Demography and was the mother of a two-and-a-half year old. In Senegal they saw another daughter, Naomi Sogie-Thomas, and her husband of twenty days. When Pat and Patty's three-week journey was over, they had touched down in nine countries and logged over 2,000 miles on some of the world's worst roads. They had had their fill of mosquitoes and heat but not of Africa's hospitality. Shortly after the trip Pat wrote in the family newsletter of "African value systems that we could well afford to study and emulate":

> For example, older people are generally treated with great respect and even with reverence. They are even more honored when they are known to be humble, honest and considerate of others. Whether they speak English well, or at all, or whether they have any money or possessions seemed to be of no importance as far as the children are concerned. Many of our CFM couples were very anxious for us to meet their humble parents, and it was a delight to see how grateful and how proud they are of these poor, old parents, who exude love and good will out of a context of little or no material goods.

That Christmas another newsletter brought the family up-to-date on other happenings. Al Augustine had married in January, and Mary Ann and Gary had had their first child, a boy named Danton, during Mom and Dad's African safari. Patrick's family of six had come to Chicago to spend Easter week with the family. Having graduated from St. Scholastica, Theresa was now enjoying the freedom of Immaculate Heart College in Los Angeles. Cathy's "on-the-job training" for Space had brought her to Afghanistan and Korea. Patsy, O.S.B., had obtained a Master's degree in theology and had escorted a group of students to a Navajo reservation in New Mexico. The family was saddened by the loss of Grandmother Marietta Caron, who died on May 17, just a year after her husband.

Pat had not composed a letter since his return from Africa, so he offered an explanation:

> To explain the delay between newsletters, the editor, i.e., the male member of the staff, was hospitalized for a few weeks in July to have a colon clog deleted. It was not a small operation, but the patient is said to look as good as he ever did (a doubtful accolade) and recovery seems complete.

What Pat was referring to so casually was his second surgery for cancer. It came two years after the first. While Patty and Patsy were awaiting the outcome of the operation, they discovered something he had written the night before on a yellow legal pad and "accidentally" left by his bedside:

> Our Lady always looks after us—Deo gratias. I'm now listening to Stravinsky, who believed in the present moment. His music elevated my consciousness to the thought that if this experience goes well, I'll be the better for it. First, more conscious of my privileges, more convinced that we have it made. St. Paul's second epistle to Timothy as interpreted by Lou Savary makes me full of confidence. What a way to be launched into this unknown! It makes me quite sure that whatever happens, 'tis the Lord's gentle always acceptable will. I'm resisting the temptation to try to figure out what makes sense because I think our dear Lord knows best. If things don't turn out as I would plan, my concern will be for the family, but I'm sure they too will have confidence that whatever is, is best and will carry on as we have with enthusiasm for each day and energy for each opportunity. There will be no more tonight lest I get pontifical, corny, and irrelevant. I face tomorrow with confidence, and that necessarily is full of hope. So back to this choice hit from WFMT and Lou Savary's most timely book.

Patty will never forget the impact of the next day. "After the operation, the intern told me the cancer was very bad. I never told Pat about it, but it always stuck in my mind. When we went to see the doctor, he said, 'It could be a long time, but it could be anytime. Put your affairs in order.' His words hit the bottom of my heart.

"Pat held in a lot, even with me sometimes. On the way home we talked about what it meant, but I felt Pat really didn't want to talk about it. Sometimes I wish we had talked a little more. A couple of times when he was sick I broke down and he got annoyed with me, really annoyed, so I just decided not to. It was hard, but why do it if it didn't make him happy?

"We both knew it was a fact, but you know how doctors are. They say someday there's going to be a cure. Then you think it's not really true. It isn't going to happen. The chemotherapy is going to work. He'll be all right."

From all outward appearances, the second occurrence of his fatal illness dampened Pat's spirit no more than the first. As he regained his strength, he poured more and more of himself into his African dream, Familia '74. It was Patty who always had managed the incredible detail of the Notre Dame convention, but this time Pat did the legwork. He submitted proposals to American foundations and asked ICCFM's correspondents to look for funds in their own countries. In September came word that the United Nations Fund for Population Activities would support Familia '74 in the amount of $74,270. In October, ICCFM met in Barcelona to coordinate details with the World Council of Churches. It was decided to have professionals film the event, and the job of raising the needed twenty thousand dollars fell to Pat. Most of it was eventually contributed by an old friend, Father Gerry Weber.

After Barcelona, planning had to be done by phone. "We had many debates with the World Council about how much money each would get and who we would bring," Patty recollects. "We wanted to bring our CFM couples because it was the first time we had gotten any money for them. They had family ministries all over the world and wanted to bring their people. So we spent two hours on the phone to Geneva, Switzerland, arguing about who was to come and who wasn't. Of course, I had this travel agency and was just dying for the business! Well, with all the arguments, the World Council of Churches decided they could get better rates. I remember the day I had to write them a fifty-thousand-dollar check. It nearly killed me."

On June 16, 1974, two hundred and fifty delegates gathered under the hot African sun to hear a blind drummer sing the praises of Tanzania at the opening of Familia '74. The congress consisted of eighty-five couples and eighty single individuals, equally divided between men and women, somewhat more from WCC than from ICCFM. All the continents and over fifty countries were represented. Among the participants from the United States were Ray and Dorothy Maldoon, Jerry and Marilyn Sexton, leaders in the St. Paul Marriage Encounter, long-time CFM chaplain Father Dennis Geaney, and two couples who had been with CFM from the very beginning, Bishop and Joyce King and Dan and Rose Lucey. Sister Patricia Crowley had been able to come, as had another Chicago nun (and a favorite of Pat's) Sister Teresita Weind.

No sooner had delegates settled into their accommodations than they were broken into groups of eight to fifteen and dispersed on buses to outlying districts of Tanzania—to Iringa and Tanga and Bagamoyo and Morogoro. There they spent two days living and working nearly forty Ujamaa villages. They made bricks, graded and packed tobacco, gathered wheat, and planted tomatoes. They exchanged songs with their hosts, witnessed school children in military drills, and posed questions through interpreters to village chiefs:

> What is the minimum age for boys and girls to get married?
> If they are not going to school, it is fifteen years.
>
> Do you have cases of interdenominational marriages?
> Yes, but not very many.
>
> How about intertribal marriages?
> These are quite numerous. My village has six or more tribes: the Hehe, Bena, Kinga, Magomba, Ngakyusa and the Nyamwezi, but what you must know is that we no longer think in terms of tribalism. We are all Tanzanians.
>
> Do young people have the freedom of choosing their partners?
> At the moment they are free but before it was the parents' duty to choose a partner for their children.
>
> Are there some polygamous marriages in your village?
> People have already started to realize the problem of having many wives and now prefer to be with one wife.
>
> Do marriages without children prosper?
> In most cases the partners stay together, trying to get treatment from traditional doctors. If this fails, they still stay together.
>
> Do you have divorcees in your village?
> Yes, both men and women. The men are more likely to remarry than women. Men, especially young ones, prefer to have young girls rather than these divorcees.
>
> Are women in your village totally emancipated?
> This sort of question is very difficult. Women in the home are subject to their husbands. For us old men it is and will always be a very difficult problem to solve. I am the one who married her and in this case she is not to rule me.
>
> Do you have cases of abortion in your village?
> Yes, but they are very rare.

Have the political changes in recent years had any effect on marriages or families?
Yes, very much. Nowadays we have to go and register our marriages, and in addition to that you can't divorce a woman without going to court; all these are great burdens to us.[1]

Between twenty and three hundred families lived in each of the Ujamaa villages, presided over by an elected chief. Most of the cooperatives were only a few years old. Lukobe, one of the smallest, was established in 1971 with only twenty-nine people on four acres. Its first harvest was twenty-four bags of maize. In 1974, however, there were seventy-five people on twenty-four acres, and the previous year's harvest had been seventy-six bags of cotton and one hundred and twenty-two bags of maize. Image, begun in 1971 with two hundred and thirty people, already had primitive facilities for blacksmithing, processing sisal, grinding maize, and packing tobacco. The villages were hardly showpieces, but they made a profound impact upon their guests from Familia '74, as a woman from Uruguay remembers:

> We played and sang with the children, seeing in each of them our own children far away. And just as we taught our own children children's songs, we taught the same songs to them; and what a joy it was to hear them sing our dear melodies, not as a colonizer teaches his language but as a brother who shares it. As a farewell from the village, and in order to show us how glad they were that we had shared in their work, they gave us a "concert."
>
> They played on two homemade marimbas to accompany themselves in singing a melody which they translated for us as "thanks to our parents for giving us life, so that we could go to visit them in Africa." Then they danced one of their native dances.
>
> When we left we gave them a present which we had brought, and they replied, "The gift has been affection which you gave us". . . . I am convinced that both they and we shall miss one another.[2]

Upon their return to the University of Dar es Salaam, delegates heard Tanzania's Muslim First Vice-President Aboud Jumbe and then entered the second phase of the conference: the Market Place. From a selection of forty seminars on communication, women's liberation, marriage enrichment, ecumenism, religious communes, human sexuality, population, development, and a dozen other topics, each person shopped for his or her favorites. Brazilian Paulo Freire, author of *Pedagogy of the Oppressed*, made three presentations, and Daniel Mbwenze and Janet Mondlane held a remarkable two-hour session on the struggle for liberation in Mozambique. There were liturgies in which the various denominations broke bread together to the singing of choirs of

Tanzanian Christians. The Market Place buzzed with ideas, confusion, and frustration, some of it due to a Pan-African Congress that had preempted space at the university.

The rest of the conference was given to drafting resolutions. They ranged from the very general, such as creating an awareness of the inequalities between the world's rich and poor, to the very specific: channeling aid to Tanzania's Community Development Trust Fund and to individual Ujamaa villages. The assembly decided to form a joint commission of ICCFM and WCC representatives to promote national and regional Familia convocations and to work for an international Familia '79 in Asia at which youth would be represented.

A position paper on the responsibilities of church bodies with regard to growing population pressure was produced for the forthcoming World Population Conference in Bucharest. The United Nations's Arthur McCormack, who helped forge the document, commented, "The thing which came out very clearly was the centrality of the couple. So often governments talk in terms of policies and family-planning people talk in terms of reductions in percentages. But when the chips are down, it is the couple that makes the decisions, and it is the couple that should have its human dignity considered. If that is done, if couples have genuine options, if they are treated with sympathy and understanding, they will play their part in helping to limit population growth. Ultimately it's men and women who have babies, not governments or churches."[3]

The strength of the two-week conference, however, was not in its resolutions or its experts, but in the bonds that were created among 250 individuals and the Ujamaa villagers. Experiences and emotions were exchanged by ordinary people in an unstructured environment. In the words of WCC's Bert Terpstra, "a theology of the small things, of problems that touch everyone in daily living," won out over a "theology of the huge abstract problems."[4]

Les Clements, who organized the assembly for the World Council, reflected at its closing, "It's very interesting in this family education area that the Protestant churches, by and large, have gone for experts. The result is a new clericalism. If a man gets a Ph. D. in the United States, he's gone back to his country as a new expert. The Church has sat back and said, 'We have an expert on family education. We will leave it to him.'

"In contrast, the Christian Family Movement began in the Roman Catholic Church, and in its beginnings strongly resisted any clerical interference and involvement. Here was the Roman Catholic Church, which we have always thought to be so priest-dominated, beginning a lay movement. The Protestant churches began a kind of priestly movement, a professional movement. I hope that out of this we will be able to move more strongly in setting up a similar, or a coordinated, movement of the laity, so that their voice is heard and that we de-professionalize the whole business."⁵

What Clements discovered through Pat Crowley and the Christian Family Movement was the original wisdom of Canon Cardijn's maxim that like was to minister to like. Thirty years before, six "guys" struggled with that formula in a Chicago law office and managed to apply it to the family. The genius of that moment had found its way, by a long and torturous route, to the hot dusty soil of Africa. In Tanzania in 1974 Pat Crowley was as enthusiastic as he had been in Chicago in 1943, riding buses, digging ditches, talking, singing, and dancing like everyone else. Never before had he brought together, in soul as well as in body, so many people of so many colors from so many places on earth. Familia '74 was the climax of his life.

When the assembly was over, and when he and Patty had paid the bills, the two did something that for them was quite extraordinary. Tired but exhilarated, they flew to London and called no one. For four days they walked around the city and enjoyed each other's company. Pat visited his favorite hat store and bought a hat, but it was no different from a dozen others he had purchased there.

Even more surprising, neither he nor Patty felt that doing absolutely nothing was a waste of time. Something in them knew that the moment had come to savor a life.

CHAPTER FOURTEEN
A TIME TO DIE

Pat and Patty with Burnie and Helene Bauer, who formed couples' groups in South Bend during World War II, at the 25th anniversary banquet of CFM, July 22, 1974.

Pat and the family in his final days.

Upon his return to the States, Pat's condition deteriorated rapidly. As his strength waned, Patty began to escort him to work and to continuing rounds of chemotherapy. "The last doctor we had was a nice older man, and he kept saying someday there's going to be a cure. But I think Pat knew that he didn't have much time."

Familia '74 was a beautiful memory, and Pat was looking forward to November, when a film of the conference, being edited in Ireland, was scheduled for completion. In July he and Patty were invited to address a meeting of the National Marriage Encounter at Barat College in Lake Forest, Illinois. The convention, ME's first as an independent national entity, opened on August 16, three weeks after a banquet commemorating the twenty-fifth anniversary of CFM. Though Pat was in pain on the evening of their talk, he and Patty donned their Familia '74 *katanga* and drove to Lake Forest in a driving rain to be Ma and Pa for one more assembly.

Pat began his rambling, light-hearted talk with a story about Tanzania, and then summed up the last quarter-century of his life: "In case any of you ever get old, I should tell you that in Tanzania they have great reverence for old age. Every place I was introduced the guy would get up and say it was wonderful that this movement had such an old man for president. I learned that was a great compliment. So if I call any of you old men, why you'll know I'm being very friendly.

"The thing that has always struck me is the enormous potential of people. This is what groups like CFM and Marriage Encounter should be concerned about—taking ordinary people, letting them feel important, and letting them develop.

"We think the movement of couples in whatever form it takes has to be outgoing. It has to be concerned with the Gospel. The thing that really enthused us in the 1940s was the twenty-fifth chapter in St. Matthew: you're going to get checked out on how you dealt with the guys who came around. Ma figured out a very simple solution to that. She decided that the way to serve the Lord when He turns up in some character is to let it be known that you like to be imposed upon. We found out very quickly that there are plenty of people who like to impose on you. It opened up all kinds of doors."

Then it was Ma's turn. These days families must get out of themselves and *act,* she said. They must open themselves to what is going on in their communities. "Families must be involved in the struggle for liberation that is going on in the world today. In Tanzania we were with families that were oppressed. We had a wonderful spirit of love and sharing there, like you do here, but a black girl from Africa was so sad after one of the liturgies because she could not go back to a free country. We went to Tanzania to awaken ourselves to what was going on. You don't know it unless you see it, and even then you don't know it. But at least you have been able to touch it a little bit."

It was their penultimate appearance as the couple who for so long had epitomized CFM. On October 7 the two spoke for the last time to a Christian Fellowship group at Chicago's Union League. An old friend of theirs happened to be in the lobby of the League and saw their name on the bulletin board. George St. Peter later wrote Patsy to describe what happened:

> I went up to the indicated room and there were Dad and Mother explaining to a group of men of various religions the technique of CFM and its strength and impact. They, and your Dad in particular, sounded just as enthusiastic and forward-sounding as they did eighteen years before. We walked to the side door on Federal Street and your mother went for the car, since your Dad could not walk very far, she said. As we were waiting, Dad said that he was in the hands of a good doctor who was doing the best he could, and he would not second-guess him. If the treatment worked, he lived; if it did not, he died. And with that we discussed the law, your family, and my family, as we always had. When he left, he was smiling and joking about something he and I always kidded about.

Before his chance meeting with St. Peter, Pat had been hospitalized for tests and medication. He chafed under the confinement of the hospital, and Patty was even more rebellious. "Pat had been there twice before, but when I came in, they made me go through an hour of telling his history. I knew he was weak and I was so afraid they were going to let him fall. Finally I got up to the room and one intern after another kept asking all these stupid questions. I got madder by the minute!

"He was supposed to stay only a few days. I was so worried that I got nurses to stay with him. The last day he didn't want to have one. I thought, 'I guess he'll be all right,' but in the middle of the night I woke up. I called the floor nurse and said, 'Be sure and watch Mr. Crowley. I'm worried about him trying to get out of bed.' They treated me as though I didn't know what I was talking about.

"Half-an-hour later they called me back. Pat had gotten up and fallen. It was four in the morning. I took a cab to the hospital, petrified. We spent most of the time in X-ray checking his head."

Pat had nothing worse than a black eye, but both he and Patty were determined to get out of the hospital. The doctor consented and Pat returned to the warmth of his home, eighty-eight floors above Chicago's lakefront.

He left only three times after that, once to address the Christian Fellowship in the Union League, again, to make an introduction for the Center for the Study of

Democratic Institutions, a third time to vote in the '74 election. In the meantime many of the people whose lives had touched his came to call. When Gene McCarthy spoke of his plans for '76, Pat endorsed them heartily, pledging his full cooperation in Illinois. Lifetime companion Ed Stephan had lunch with him in late September and found him "quite hopeful of making it." A few weeks later, Stephan and his wife Evie returned for a dinner party with journalist John Cogley and friends Bill and Nancy Dreux. At that point Pat "looked as if he were dying, but he was his same lovable self. He came in, sat down, and joked a lot. He took part in everything. I think he wanted to live because he felt there was so much more to do."

His children were with him too, even those from his extended family. Mary Ann "never thought he'd die. Even when he was sick, he never complained. Just kept smiling and trying to be happy." Cathy came to the apartment to play on the piano the music he loved to hear, and Patsy cherished the moments when he revealed to her ever more of what he was:

"I was taking a dream course at the Y and used to visit him at the hospital on the way home. He wanted to know what I was learning so he told me his dreams. There was a crazy dream I've often thought about—something he knew about the Kennedy's that nobody else knew. The government was trying to find out, but he wasn't about to tell them. There was a hidden treasure and all this chase. It was the kind of thing that made me wonder if his mind didn't work a lot the whole time.

"His dreams were struggling dreams. I'm not sure he was that inwardly placid. I don't think he could have done all he did for people just off the cuff. Too much came out of him, too many angles to everything. He was always getting ideas, constantly creating new things. Lots of times I can remember him saying, 'I've got the best idea. What do you think of this?' He did that with my mother all the time. Inside, he was always working.

"Still, deep inside him, there was that traditional Irish faith. He went to daily mass most of his life. When he first found out his sickness was terminal, he told me that if it weren't for my mother he would go into a monastery for a couple of months. He was half-kidding but he was serious too. I was touched because it said he valued the inner life. One night when he was sick I prayed the rosary with him. I'm not sure I'd do that with my mother. I've never seen a rosary around her side of the bed but I did around my father's. My mother is very able to understand my youngest sisters' not going to church, but my father found that hard to understand. It really bothered him.

"When he came home from the hospital, he let me do a lot of things for him. He let me give him a shower, do his toenails, and that kind of thing. It meant a lot to me. I think it was his way of saying that he was okay, that we were okay too. I could do something for him and we could be all right after.

"Sometimes I regret I never asked if he wanted to tell me something, and yet it just wasn't in keeping with who he was to say, 'What words of wisdom do you have?' His whole life was wisdom to us. There were a couple of times when I was alone with him, and I was so tempted, but I just couldn't bring myself to do it. I think I was almost afraid that he didn't want to, that there wasn't a last word."

Another to whom Pat opened himself was Dr. Jack Graller, a psychiatrist and a friend from the Family Institute. Graller later recalled their last conversation in a letter to Patty:

> Pat's concerns were how to best care for the family, and after some moments of talking about "practical" caring, I wondered if he was more (or really) concerned about how he could "take care of the family" emotionally. He wanted to protect you from his emotional pain, from his fear of the inevitable. He wanted to give, but didn't have the strength anymore; he thought he'd have to be physically strong to give—a true misconception. I asked, "What haven't you already given?" There was a long silence . . . we both struggled with the answer, and we arrived at the answer together.
>
> There were some corners of his personality that you had only seen glimpses of—the part of him that *wasn't* in control. When the control was silence, evasiveness or humor, as only he could do, you weren't seeing the inner man. He struggled with the idea of *taking* from you and the kids in a passive way, as a way of giving you part of himself. So he decided that, for once, he could be passive and receptive—out-of-control for him—and let you take care of him, love him, without his having to be strong. He wanted to give you that—along with a chance to know him in a different way—when he was facing death.
>
> I encouraged him to give you something else—to show his strength by teaching you and the children how to say good-bye; how to be courageous, and stoic, and to not be afraid to be (and show) his fears. I hope he had enough strength and time in his last days to verbalize some of these things. He knew his time was short.
>
> He loved you all dearly, and feared that he would not be able to speak clearly to you at the end.

Patty knew that her husband wasn't "showy" in his religion, but she "always felt his inner feelings for the Lord were very, very deep." Outwardly strong because that was what he wanted, she began to pray the Psalms with him, one each day. As their thirty-seventh wedding anniversary came and passed, it became clear that his time was coming close, so she called her children home. Theresa flew in from the West Coast and Patrick and his family from the East. The clan gathered in the apartment on the evening of November 2 for the Mass of the Anointing of the Sick. Father Robert McLaughlin explained that the rite had replaced what was once known as the last sacraments.

It was during that mass that Pat came closest to expressing a last word. No one remembers exactly what his prayer was—a thanksgiving for life, joy in the present moment of togetherness, blessings upon his family, sorrow at his departure. Whatever it was that he began to utter he could not finish. His emotions overwhelmed him, and for the first time in his life, he wept in the presence of his family.

In the days following his anointing Pat regained his sense of fun. He wrote Paul VI to nominate Argentinian Helder Camara for pope and was amused at the reply of a Vatican bureaucrat. Encouraging his family to laugh at his incapacities, he spoke in a final conversation with Ed Stephan of "goofy" illusions—trying to call the Curia and not getting through, seeing Ma and Mayor Daley coming down a river on a boat under a shower of fireworks.

In the meantime Patty was pulling strings to speed along the Familia '74 film. She told the producers how sick her husband was, and found an Irish CFM couple whose son was a pilot for Irish Airlines. When the film was finished, the son asked a friend flying to Chicago to take the film with him, and the friend delivered it personally to the Crowley apartment. Then Pat said he didn't want to see it until he was in the right mood.

By Sunday, November 17, he still wasn't ready, and his consciousness was lapsing. Patsy was with him that morning. "Mom wanted him to see the movie, and I struggled with myself because I had a sense that he didn't want to see it. But I did it for her. I brought the projector into the bedroom and set up a sheet because he couldn't possibly have gotten up. He saw it. I think he knew what was going on and was moved by it. Mom's not sure he did, but I sense that he did."

On Wednesday morning the doctor came to the apartment and said Pat would die by nightfall. On that day Patty had come to Psalm 34: "I seek Yahweh, and he answers me and frees me from all my fears. . . . How good Yahweh is—only taste and see! Happy the man who takes shelter in him."

Throughout the day visitors who called were brought to Pat's bedside and by evening the family who remained were prepared for the end. Theresa had been unable to return from Los Angeles, and Al was detained in downstate Illinois, but Patrick was on his way from Baltimore. At ten o'clock he opened the door of the apartment. Not knowing his father had only minutes to live, he ran into the bedroom, sized up the situation, and cried frantically, "Call a doctor!"

It was a quirk. It was *lila*. His words ignited the tension and the room exploded with laughter. Everyone—suddenly, unabashedly, and in unison—cracked up.

When the noise subsided, and when the family relaxed for the first time that day, Pat took a deep breath and slept peacefully away. Those at his side say he had chosen the moment.

Almost without words it was understood that the next few days would be an affirmation of life. The wake was held not in a funeral parlor, but at home. When the morticians pulled the drapes shut to give the living room an air of solemnity, Patty reopened them to the glory of the city outside. Day and night she remained with the crowds who came to pay their respects. The well-known appeared, and so did the humble, people of all religions and colors laughing and weeping together, amazed at Patty's stamina. "I did very little crying and the children had a hard time understanding it. But Pat didn't want me to. I felt very close to him, I must say. He was pushing me to go ahead. When I did things, I felt he was doing them with me."

While Patty welcomed guests in the front of the apartment, the children were in the back planning the funeral. For the cover of the booklet for the Mass of the Resurrection, Collette used black ink on a pale yellow background to etch her feelings: light radiating in all directions from a single point, and above it the words, "Let Us Join Together In Prayer, Let Us Celebrate Pat's Life."

Pat's life had first brushed Patty's some forty years before at a crowded *Tre Ore* service in Holy Name Cathedral. It was there, on November 23, 1974, a warm, clear day offering a distant promise of spring, that the meaning of their union was proclaimed.

"I am the resurrection and the life," the congregation began, and their singing burst the seams of the building. "I am the resurrection and the life. He who believes in me will live a new life." As priests in white vestments moved among the stately pillars of the sanctuary, a young man stepped beneath a huge, yellow banner that announced, "Service to the Lord, Service to the City, Service to the People." He began to sing:

> To everything,
> There is a season,
> And a time for every purpose under heaven.
>
> A time to be born, a time to die.
> A time to plant, a time to reap.
> A time to kill, a time to heal.
> A time to laugh, a time to reap.

Men and women, young and old, light and dark, read alone and together. "Which of you wants to live to the full?" one quoted the Psalms. "Who loves long life and enjoyment of prosperity?" The people responded, "I will praise the Lord no matter what happens." Another declared, "From the beginning till now the entire creation, as we know, has been groaning in one great act of giving birth. We too groan inwardly as we wait for our bodies to be set free." "Alleluia, alleluia, alleluia," came the reply. Still another read from the Gospels:

> How happy are the poor in spirit:
>   theirs is the kingdom of heaven.
> Happy the gentle:
>   they shall have the earth for their heritage.
> Happy those who mourn:
>   they shall be comforted.
> Happy those who hunger and thirst for what is right:
>   they shall be satisfied.
> Happy the merciful:
>   they shall have mercy shown them.
> Happy the pure in heart:
>   they shall see God.
> Happy the peacemakers:
>   they shall be called sons of God.

To the pulpit came a bishop vested in white. He spoke of a man who was the precursor of a new kind of Catholic layman, who took to heart the words Pius XII uttered in 1943, "You are the Church." He related the origins and impact of a simple formula, "Observe-Judge-Act," and described a popular movement that touched the lives of families from Maine to California, from Uruguay to Japan to Tanzania.

Then from an alcove came the voices of women singing of wisdom building a house, preparing a table, bringing forth wine, calling her children to a feast. "They have come from eastern and western lands, gathered around your table at the feast of the kingdom." Gifts of bread and wine were offered by students from around the world, each bedecked in the dress of his or her homeland. The mass moved on through stillness and song, approached its sacred core, then called forth five resounding amens. The people turned to one another, clasped hands, and exchanged a greeting of peace. Then they moved up the aisle.

> Shalom, chaverim, shalom, chaverim,
> Shalom, shalom,
> Le hitraot, le hitraot,
> Shalom, shalom.
>
> I am the bread of life.
> He who comes to me shall not hunger.
> He who believes in me shall not die.
> No one can come to me unless the Father send him.
> And I will raise him up,
> And I will raise him up,
> And I will raise him up on the last day.

The silence that followed was broken by the tones of an autoharp and the piercing voice of a slight black woman in a long robe of orange, black, and tan. Strong, confident, pure, her notes ascended, lifting the people with them. Higher still she took them, and when she climaxed in a string of alleluias, the faces of many were wet with tears. "The sister was singing out all the love she had for Pat," someone wrote later, "and singing the love and gratitude for everybody in the church."

It was nearly over. A man of prominence, a onetime presidential candidate, arose and spoke of a modern-day saint who had the ability to understand and love the poor and, something far harder, to understand and love the rich. This man neither hoarded his wealth nor felt guilty because of it. He knew the place of possessions—how to have enough, but not too much, how to share what he had. A happy man, a man of compassion, he was never too busy or tired to counsel one more person, promote one more cause, join one more organization. He spent his life preaching the Gospel to the rich.

Finally, the people stood and prepared to leave. It was a difficult moment. A refrain was begun, the melody the Shaker hymn, "Simple Gifts." It faltered, but as the congregation moved slowly down the aisle, it gained in strength and sealed the meaning of what had taken place.

> I danced in the morning when the world was begun,
> And I danced in the moon and the stars and the sun,
> And I came down from heaven and I danced on the earth.
> At Bethlehem I had my birth.

> Dance, then, wherever you may be.
> I am the Lord of the Dance, said He.
> I'll lead you all, wherever you may be,
> I will lead you all in the dance, said He.

The bright sun stung eyes as the casket, covered in white, was carried from the church and lifted into a hearse. Cars formed a line and drove silently between the tall buildings of downtown Chicago. Turning left, they moved along Lake Shore Drive, the outline of the city on one side, the broad expanse of Lake Michigan on the other. Slowly clouds gathered, as if to absorb the burden from below. By the time the procession reached the gravesite, a few drops of rain had become a downpour, and all the grief and sorrow were released. It rained and rained and rained. As Pat Crowley was laid to rest beneath a statue of St. Patrick, one of his family remarked, "Daddy must be laughing at us, standing here in all this rain."

The family continues to gather: Patty's 65th birthday, Rochelle, Illinois, 1978.

EPILOGUE

"T.C." at twenty-one.

They dance on.

At twenty-one, "T.C." is the youngest, and the abbot always made a point of taking counsel from the youngest. "He would always ask me what I thought, and I would always say I don't know. The youngest was very young!

"When I was thirteen, I rebelled. You're supposed to at thirteen. Whatever Dad did, I did the opposite. I said, 'I'm not going to church anymore because I don't see the point of it.' Dad's whole thing was public celebration: we're in the same predicament and we're going to worship God and we're going to do it together. He'd be ready to go to church and I'd still be sleeping. He'd come into my room. 'AHEM, well, we're going to church, Theresa. You ready?' I'd say, 'I'm not going.' 'Well, we'll see you there, okay?' That's as far as he went. There were a couple of times when he said, 'Hey, I just can't understand it. If you could tell me.' But I was never very good at telling.

"I never felt very much inside his head. I never knew what he was thinking. The older I got, the more I could sense his different moods. But he was so happy and so jovial that I thought, 'Here he is Santa Claus all the time.' He had one great song:

> Oh, give us a drink bartender, bartender,
> For we love you as you know,
> And surely you'll oblige us, oblige us
> With another drink or so.
> And when we get drunk,
> Just roll us in the bunk,
> Cause it's nobody's business but our own.
> Nobody's business, nobody's business,
> Nobody's business but our own.

Then he'd make a long 'Oh-h-h-h-h-h' and start all over. I made him sing it all the time. Once I told him to sing it and said, 'Wait, wait, I have to get ready.' I laid down on the floor and got ready to roll around and laugh.

"Yet I wish so much wasn't hidden from us. He worried about how he could show us there were bad things in life and still protect us from them. When I was really young, I'd go and sing songs for the old folks in the ghetto. So I knew that everyone didn't have it the way I did. When I got home, Dad wouldn't say, 'Now don't worry about it. That will never happen to you.' He'd let us see these things, but still he wanted to protect us. He did that, I think, by never letting us see him down. As long as he was fine, everything was fine.

"He never wanted to dwell on something bad. What can you do about it? Nothing. That's another reason why a lot was hidden. But I wish I had known sometimes. A lot of times I wish he had taken me aside and said, 'You're being a little brat. Cool it.' But he couldn't because he always believed that I had a lot of potential and that I'd be a good person. He let my whole life take its course.

"When he was dying, he talked to a psychiatrist from the Family Institute and said, 'How do I prepare them for this? What do I say to them? What can I do?' After he died, the doctor wanted to tell us what he was thinking because Dad hadn't told us, so he sent us a letter. He said that Dad knew his place, that his place was a high one, and that there were going to be a lot of adjustments.

"I've been able to verbalize my views only in the last two years. I've decided now that if I do everything consciously as a service to God, that's a prayer, that's worship. So lately my whole life has been centered on centering myself on God, saying I'm part of the flow of God. But I never got the chance to talk to Dad about it.

"A while before he died, I told him I was changing from an art major to an English major. He said, 'Good, because communication is the most important thing in the world.' Then, when I took a class in Theater of the Absurd, I came home and said, 'Dad, I'm an existentialist. That's the only way to do it: be a total existentialist.' And he said, 'Oh, really? Well, I'm a humanist.' I wasn't going to find out till next semester what a humanist was, so I said, 'What's a humanist?' and he answered, 'One who believes in the potential of the human.' I said, 'I'll see about that, Dad,' and he dropped me off at the airport.

"When I came back, I was going to read him some plays by Samual Beckett because he loved *Waiting for Godot*. He was sitting in that chair and I started reading, but he just kept falling asleep. So I said, 'Well, forget it. Go back to your room and lie down.'

"The night of the wake he was out in the living room and I couldn't sleep. I didn't know what to do, so I got up and washed my hair. My sister was sleeping. I came out, and the casket was there. I stayed away from it. I just sat there and said, 'Well, you've got a lot of pull now, so do something. Send up signs. Do all these wonderful things.' Then I'd say, 'I'm really stupid! I'm sitting here talking to this dead body.' So I'd run into the other room and I'd lie down, and come back out, and each time I'd get closer until finally I was just sitting there saying, 'Well, you know you're going to be watching.' And I had this great vision that he was going to be on my right-hand shoulder for the rest of my life. I thought, 'Okay, I'm being watched over.' And things got much easier then.

"After that was my Thanksgiving vacation. I could have stayed, but I left because I had figured out how I was going to deal with it. I felt good because . . . it may not have been the best way of handling the situation, but at least I wasn't saying, 'What am I going to do with my life? This person is gone.' I found out later that was a pretty Eastern way of handling the whole thing. It's done, he's gone, but he's here and we go on.

"Since then unbelievable things have happened. I'm a straight A-B student. Before it was C's and D's. I've finished a major and a half already and I'm going to finish two majors. I used to run away from everything, but now I say 'That's not the way to do it. You face everything head-on 'cause you can beat it. You're bigger than it.' Sometimes I feel it's unfortunate he isn't seeing this progress. But he is. He's on my shoulder, every day, every night. I feel I'm so much of him, so much of him is me!

"Last night I went through some books and, you know, I *know* these people. My father's read these books. I know the same poets as he. I'm probably not really Irish, but I have this great feeling of Irish heritage. I'm tied closely to the past, just as he was.

"If I hadn't rebelled, I wonder if I would ever have delved into religion, looking for the purity in it rather than the ornamentation. I would probably be a good Catholic, going to confession and communion, but I don't think I would have had the chance to expand. One of the things I brought home to read is the *Gita*. I'm also reading Meher Baba and Baba Ram Dass and looking through Hindu literature. There have been a lot of people in California who have influenced me, but Dad's been there the whole time.

"The main example I have of how to live my own life is how my parents lived their lives, which does not include the fact that just because they were in the institutional Church, I have to be in that institutional Church. You know, they were sacred people. They were really holy. Anyone who wanted to came into our house, and there was always an extra placesetting at the dinner table for the person who came unexpectedly. And that's just my life, basically. My philosophy is patterned after theirs."

I spoke with T.C. where I spoke with so many of the people whose lives were affected by the Crowleys, in the apartment where Pat died. On cold, snowy days that apartment is enveloped in a cocoon of clouds, a warm, secure refuge in a city of concrete and steel. On sunny, summer afternoons there is often comedy outside the windows: small airplanes darting about or a huge blimp bobbing straight at you like a fish in an aquarium. The atmosphere here is unpretentious, informal, hospitable, a backyard eighty-eight stories above the ground. The phone rings constantly and a steady stream of visitors comes in, stays for an hour or two, and then moves on. I interview some of them in the back bedroom. I help myself to lunch at the same table over which so much of CFM's early business was transacted. Patty departs for an engagement and I am left alone to pore over old issues of *Act,* newspaper clippings, scrapbooks, hundreds and hundreds of letters paying tribute to Pat. That evening there is a dinner for some students just arrived from Italy, for the president couple of CFM, and for a foreign student who first lived with the Crowleys twenty years before. She has brought her children and will stay a few days so they can get to know "Mom." Things *happen* here, new things, but they are still infused with the memory of Pat.

Patty has not found it easy adjusting to his absence. On rare occasions when there are no guests or children in the apartment she misses him acutely. Yet she knows she must continue to act as the two of them did in the past. And so she does: helping Vietnamese refugees, planning the ICCFM convention that met in the Philippines in 1977, participating in important lay developments like the Detroit Call to Action and the Chicago Declaration of Christian Concern. As president of Space, she led one of the first travel groups to visit the reopened mainland of China, and she has led subsequent tours of Italy, Egypt, and Poland. She has continued to serve the International Visitors Center, the American Indian Center, the Family Institute, and the United Nations Association, and she has taken Pat's place on the board of Caron International. She also sits on the board of the First Security Bank and heads the Friends of the Chicago Public Library. She knew from the moment Pat was buried that she would have to steel herself to carry on. When New Years' eve came she made herself and Cathy visit the family of one of the first foreign students to stay with them. It was difficult but it was better than sitting at home with the memory of past New Years. She attended political parties, alone, out of loyalty to Pat. She accepted awards in his honor, though she fought tears to do so. Invited to Belgium for a meeting on men and women in Christian community and to Rome for a Congress of the Laity, she experienced how painful it was to do as a widow things she and Pat had done together, to see old friends but have no one with whom to talk intimately. Gradually she learned that it was better to get involved in altogether new endeavors.

"Since Pat died I can't believe what I've been asked to do. And yet . . . why would you be asked? I feel very much that I should keep doing them. I feel Pat is pushing me on. 'Don't be silly, don't be moping,' he's saying. He would have me do it and he's helping me do it. For example, I was asked to give a talk on the family at the Eucharistic Congress. I wasn't capable of doing that. Anybody who knows me knows that I wasn't. But somehow I got help from other people and I did it."

Her children and grandchildren mean more and more to Patty, and so does a community of widows, single women, and nuns. Patty is working with one group in Chicago to define the role of laywomen in the Church. At the same time she and Patsy are active in the national women's ordination movement. As she becomes aware of the injustices suffered by single women, women's issues increasingly become her own. She has written in support of the Equal Rights Amendment. She has refused to give talks on married spirituality and has spoken instead on widowhood. "Pat always said the real heroines of the Church are the religious women who have done so much in community life. They really listened to Vatican II." She intends to bring that idea of community to more single women.

After the strenuous meeting in the Philippines, Patty stepped down as president of ICCFM. But she believes as strongly as ever in the idea behind the movement and she works regularly with its leaders. If the Inquiry Method were properly applied, she insists, it would work as well in the seventies and eighties as it did in the forties, fifties, and sixties. Families cannot be concerned with themselves alone; nor can single persons. Things open up if you keep yourself open, so you have to plunge right in. When I first spoke with Patty in 1976 she herself had just started a local action group. It was only a tiny seed and she thought to mention it only because she was reminiscing about the euphoria of the first groups in the late forties. She had just seen that spirit rekindled. "The young couples were so thrilled that they could go and say hello to somebody they didn't know in their office or their building. One couple seven floors down talked about a lonely old woman who had asked them to come over. They had never gone. They started to think, 'Well, maybe you have to go out of your way. Maybe just going to call on this woman would mean so much to her.' We started them right out with an action. They're going to go this week."

NOTES

Chapter 1

"The Lay Apostolate," translated in London by the Catholic Truth Society; quoted in Daniel Callahan, *The Mind of the Catholic Layman* (New York: Charles Scribner's Sons, 1963), p. 106.

Chapter 5

1. Joseph Cardijn, *Laymen in Action* (London: Geoffrey Chapman, 1964), all quotations p.28.
2. Ibid., p. 30.
3. Ibid., p. 40.
4. Andrew Greeley, "The Chicago Experience" in *The Catholic Experience* (Garden City, N. Y.: Doubleday, 1967) describes the activities of three decades of Chicago liberals; Daniel Callahan, *The Mind of the Catholic Layman* (New York: Charles Scribner's Sons, 1963) places in historical perspective the surge of American Catholic lay activity that began in the 1930s.

Chapter 9

1. The *National Catholic Reporter*, April 19, 1967, p. 1.
2. Ibid.
3. Ibid., August 7, 1968, p. 8.
4. Ibid.
5. The *Chicago Sun-Times*, August 11, 1968, section 4, p. 1.
6. The *National Register*, August 11, 1968, p. 1.

Chapter 12

1. *Act*, September, 1962.
2. *The St. Louis Review*, 1965.
3. All quotations from *Act*, December, 1965-January, 1966.
4. *Act*, July, 1965, p. 2.
5. *Act*, May, 1966, pp. 6-7.
6. Quoted by John L. Giannini, "An Historical and Psychological Study of the Christian Family Movement," unpublished paper, August, 1969, p. 65.
7. *Act*, February, 1970, p. 1.
8. *Act*, December, 1970-January, 1971, p. 1.

9. The data upon which this paragraph is based may be found in Andrew M. Greeley, William C. McCready, and Kathleen McCourt, *Catholic Schools in a Declining Church* (Kansas City: Sheed and Ward, 1976).

Chapter 13

1. Condensed from a report by Francis A. Lubowa, a Familia '74 participant from Uganda, published in *Risk*, a journal of the World Council of Churches, vol. 10, no. 4, pp. 21-22.
2. Nelly C. de Aniano in *Risk*, vol. 10, no. 4, p. 24.
3. From a tape-recorded account of Familia '74 prepared by Bert Terpstra.
4. Ibid.
5. Ibid.